W9-BPS-276

RIGHTS

Theodore M. Benditt

Rights are everywhere in contemporary moral and political debate. We claim constitutional rights to speak and worship freely, to associate freely, to own guns. We have a right to vote, a right to life, and, some would say, a right to die. A few years ago the right to a paid vacation was proclaimed; today there is talk of a right to health care, to a minimum standard of living, and to a job.

In this book, Theodore Benditt examines the many different aspects of the question of rights: what are they, do they have historical precedent, are they a part of our moral thinking, are they absolute? Discussing in detail various theories of rights, he addresses the thorny issue of general rights and why they come into conflict with one another. He also assesses what rights people actually have against other people and against society, and includes arguments about the state of nature in moral thinking and the role of rights in law.

For a note on the author, see the back flap

RIGHTS

PHILOSOPHY AND SOCIETY
General Editor: Marshall Cohen

Also in this series:

ETHICS IN THE WORLD OF BUSINESS
David Braybrooke

MARX AND JUSTICE
THE RADICAL CRITIQUE OF LIBERALISM
Allen E. Buchanan

LUKÁCS, MARX AND THE SOURCES OF CRITICAL THEORY
Andrew Feenberg

THE REVERSE DISCRIMINATION CONTROVERSY
A MORAL AND LEGAL ANALYSIS
Robert K. Fullinwider

THE MORAL FOUNDATIONS OF PROFESSIONAL ETHICS
Alan H. Goldman

THE LIBERTARIAN READER
Tibor R. Machan (ed.)

READING NOZICK
Jeffrey Paul (ed.)

AND JUSTICE FOR ALL
NEW INTRODUCTORY ESSAYS IN ETHICS AND PUBLIC POLICY
Tom Regan and Donald VanDeVeer (eds.)

EVOLUTIONARY EXPLANATION IN THE SOCIAL SCIENCES
AN EMERGING PARADIGM
Philippe Van Parijs

RIGHTS

THEODORE M. BENDITT

ROWMAN AND LITTLEFIELD
Totowa, New Jersey

First published in the United States 1982 by Rowman and Littlefield,
81 Adams Drive, Totowa, New Jersey 07512.

Library of Congress Cataloging in Publication Data

Benditt, Theodore M.
  Rights.

  (Philosophy and society)
  Bibliography: p.
  Includes index.
  1. Civil rights. I. Title. II. Series.
JC571.B46   1982   323.4'01   81-23448
ISBN 0-8476-6754-5   AACR2

Distributed in the U.K. and Commonwealth by
George Prior Associated Publishers Limited
High Holborn House
53154 High Holborn
London WC1 V 6RL
England

Printed in the United States of America

To my wife Anne,
who inspires me

Table of Contents

Acknowledgments ix

1 Introduction 1

2 Utilitarianism and Rights 20

3 On Having a Right 34

4 Rights and the Duty to Compensate 51

5 The Right to Beneficence 65

6 Intuitionism 81

7 Rights Against Society 100

8 Rights in Law 122

References 143

Index 146

Acknowledgments

I would like to thank Malcolm Acock, George Graham, William Nelson, Gregory Pence, James Rachels, and Carl Wellman, all of whom were kind enough to read and comment on various chapters of this book.

I am grateful to the students in my seminar on rights at the University of Pittsburgh in the Fall of 1979, who helped me think through many of the issues discussed here.

Most importantly, I want to thank my wife Anne, whose support in this project has been immensely valuable.

T.M.B.

1

Introduction

The Importance of Rights

Rights are everywhere in contemporary moral and political debate. We claim Constitutional rights to speak and worship freely, to associate freely, and some claim a right to own guns. We have a right to vote, to our vote being worth as much as another person's vote, to an education, and to equal educational opportunity. Of course, we have a right to life, and some would say a right to die, or at least a right to die with dignity. Strange sounding rights like the right of a criminal to be punished have been asserted. There is serious debate today over whether there is a right to health care, a right to a minimum standard of living, and a right to a job—even a right to a satisfying job. A number of years ago a right to a vacation with pay was proclaimed, and nowadays rights to clean air and water are demanded. Some people contend that non-human animals have rights, and others contend that children have more rights than are usually recognized. Even a right to have a pet, or to have money to support one included in a social minimum, has been pushed, while at the other end of the rights spectrum rights to personhood, to equality, and to self-development and self-realization have been urged.

It's a strange thing that rights play so important a role in moral and political thought whereas historically they have not always done so. The Greeks and Romans did not press rights on one another—they didn't think in those terms. Indeed, they didn't really seem to have had the idea of a personal right, and even though there are some suggestions to the contrary in some Roman writings, there certainly was not a well understood notion of rights that was part of the common language of the time. It appears that by the early thirteenth century the idea of rights in some sense was around (Magna Carta, in 1215, speaks of *iura:* rights), but it was not until the fourteenth century that there is evidence of an attempt to define the notion. Such an effort is attributed to William of Ockham: "Natural right is nothing other than a power to conform to right reason, without an agreement or pact; civil right is a power, deriving from an agreement, and sometimes conforms to right reason and sometimes discords with it." (See Golding, 1978, 48.)

By the eighteenth century the idea of personal rights was well entrenched, playing an important role in law and in the political thought of the American colonies and in France. But now one might well ask, were there no personal rights prior to, say, the thirteenth century? If there were, then we must come to the awkward conclusion that people were not aware of them; but if there were not, then we seem to come to the equally awkward conclusion that rights come into existence only when people become aware of the concept.

There is a body of thought which regards both of these alternatives as mistaken. On this view any idea belongs to a historical period; it is born of the conditions of that period. The idea of a right comes out of an era which saw the rise of the nation-state, and, as a concomitant, the rise of the individual, the citizen, a morally self-contained atom shorn of all of the ties of family, class, and status which for so long defined people and their moral and social situations. The possession of a personal right means that people think of themselves as distinct from others, as having interests that differ from the interests of others. But such a state of affairs occurs only where people establish their outlooks on life, their needs and desires, independently of others, and in which they are shorn from the webs of relationships that once played those formative roles. It is only when a society becomes thus unglued, when people become unattached and the only status available to them is that of citizen, such that they are opposed to and in competition with others, that rights have a role. So on this view the notion of a right is seen as a phenomenon of a particular set of historical changes, and it has a point only so long as those circumstances still define the social world. It is the view of some historicists that, as the nation-state and its concomitant the isolated citizen are bad ideas, the time of rights has passed, and that the idea of rights is now an anachronism we should forget about.

We cannot go further into the set of ideas sketched above, and it is for the reader to decide whether the idea of rights still has life in it. It may be that the eighteenth century had a particular view of rights which has changed over time—ideas, after all, change too. And besides, it is hardly clear just how closely ideas are wed to conditions and circumstances, and so we may be able to, and find good reason to, *choose* to fashion for ourselves a notion of rights that seems useful. What we come up with may bear enough relation to older ideas of rights that we can plausibly say that what we have is a notion of *rights*.

If we wish to determine whether we can come up with a useful notion of rights, we are immediately faced with the question "Why bother?" After all, the ancients and the medievals did not have the notion of a right—was their moral life stunted in some way as a result? Did they lack the tools for dealing with certain aspects of the moral enterprise? Among them moral questions were dealt with in terms of what is right or wrong, what is in accordance with or required by the natural law, what people ought to do or are obliged to do, but not in terms of what someone has *a* right to, or has *a* right to do.

Some philosophers have recently argued that the lack of the concept of a right does impoverish a morality. It will be profitable in this regard to discuss the important paper of Joel Feinberg, "The Nature and Value of Rights" (1970). In this paper Feinberg asks us to think about an imaginary place called Nowheresville in which no one has any rights. Nowheresville is not represented as a bad place—indeed, on the whole it is a very good place, for there is still the idea of right and wrong behavior, and people are well disposed toward doing what is right. There is benevolence, compassion, sympathy, and pity. Furthermore, people in Nowheresville have and act on the idea of duty, in the broad sense of something that is required of them. But in keeping with the limitations on Nowheresville, the duties that people there have do not correlate with rights—that is, their duties are not owed to determinate individuals who are personally entitled to the fulfillment of those duties. Accordingly, the duties existing in Nowheresville are, largely, duties of obedience to law (insofar as these duties are not owed to anyone in particular) and duties of charity. There is, in addition, the idea that people sometimes deserve rewards (or penalties) as fitting responses to certain acts. If someone finds and returns my watch, he deserves a reward, but he does not thereby have a right to one.

There is one more important element in the moral life of Nowheresvillians, which Feinberg calls a "sovereign monopoly of rights." There must be, after all, some rights in Nowheresville, for we cannot come to grips with the notion of a contract, a promise, marriage, property, and others without the idea of a right, for promises (to take one example) can't be understood without the idea of someone's having a duty to keep a promise, a duty which is owed to someone, for a duty to keep a promise is not like a duty to give to charity. Very well, Feinberg says, let's introduce rights, but "with one big twist." Let's imagine that duties like the duty to keep a promise are owed not to the beneficiary of the promise, but to a third party—perhaps God, or the king. Thus it is God to whom I make the promise to do things for your benefit, and so my duty to keep my promise is owed not to you, but to God. If I fail to keep my promise I have wronged not you, but God, and you have no claim on me to fulfill my promise.

Nowheresvillians are rather better than we are in acting decently, and so on the whole it's a pretty good place. Nevertheless there is, Feinberg believes, something important missing from the moral life of this community—the idea that a person is entitled to something, can claim something, as his own due. "Nowheresvillians, even when they are discriminated against invidiously, or otherwise badly treated, do not think to leap to their feet and make righteous demands against one another. . . ." (Feinberg, 1970, 249) But this is, as Feinberg sees it, exactly the crux of the notion of rights; in lacking rights, what Nowheresvillians lack is exactly that sense of making claims on their own behalf.

Feinberg's argument, then, is two-fold. First, that rights are distinctive in morality, the argument for which we have just seen: rights, and only rights, make possible the claiming of something in one's own name. Second, rights are valuable—they provide something that should exist in a community's morality. For

having rights enables us to "stand up like men," to look others in the eye, and to feel in some fundamental way the equal of anyone. To think of oneself as the holder of rights is . . . to have that minimal self-respect that is necessary to be worthy of the love and esteem of others. Indeed, respect for persons . . . may simply be respect for their rights . . . and what is called "human dignity" may simply be the recognizable capacity to assert claims. (Feinberg, 1970, 252)

Thus, since rights provide things of moral value, and since only rights can provide those things, a morality without rights is incomplete.

Despite the initial plausibility of this argument, it is not really convincing. First of all let's be sure we understand what is missing in Nowheresville. A lot of what Feinberg says makes it seem that it is a world of docile, accepting individuals. For example, in his discussion of desert Feinberg says that in Nowheresville teachers grading students and judges awarding prizes will usually try to give students and contestants the grades and prizes they deserve, and that "for this the recipients will be grateful; but they will never think to complain, or even feel aggrieved, when the expected responses to desert fail. . . . One should be happy that they *ever* treat us well, and not grumble over their occasional lapses." (Feinberg, 1970, 247) There is also the remark quoted previously about people in Nowheresville not thinking "to leap to their feet." And in a 'postscript' to his article Feinberg suggests that the word 'servile' applies to Nowheresvillians. (Feinberg, 1977, 32)

But it would be a mistake to read Feinberg as saying that a world without rights is a world of bowing and scraping, in which people can only say "thank you" for not hurting them. For there is no reason why Nowheresvillians must stand idly by without complaining. One can complain about someone's failure to give a deserved reward, of a failure to fulfill a duty no matter to whom it is owed, of a failure of benevolence, compassion, pity, and all the rest. Feinberg could, indeed, include complaining in the moral world of the Nowheresvillians. All that he needs to exclude is people complaining in the name of themselves or of any other person. I could, for example, say "You've done wrong; do what's right," without implying that you owed the performance to me or to anyone else; I would not be *claiming* it of you on my, or someone else's, behalf.

But while people in Nowheresville do not lack the capacity to complain, they do lack the capacity to claim. What they are thus missing is a sense of self, of status, of something being owed them—which are connected with the notion of claiming.

Is Nowheresville deficient because of this? Would it be a good thing to introduce claiming into that moral community? Well, it is certainly a very bad thing not to be able to make claims when others are able to do so, for then one is decidedly inferior in status. But that's not the problem in Nowheresville. The question is not whether some should be able to make claims while others aren't, but whether everyone (rather than no one) should be able to do so. In trying to answer this question, we must be aware that the recognition of rights is not all gain. Some people do gain in having a personal status they can call upon others to honor. But the very existence of this status can *get in the way* of the fulfillment of duty, in two ways. First, some people sometimes resist doing their duty because it implies the recognition of another's status. Feinberg himself gives an excellent example. When Bobby kicks Billy, he may be willing to apologize to Daddy, but "a direct apology to Billy would be a tacit recognition of Billy's status as a right-holder against him, someone he can wrong as well as harm, and someone to whom he is directly accountable for his wrongs. This is a status Bobby will happily accord Daddy, but it would imply a respect for Billy that he does not presently feel. . . ." (Feinberg, 1970, 248) The second way is related. People often try to establish dominance over others, and one way to do this is to refuse deliberately to come forward with something to which another person is entitled. Not only is a loss thus imposed, but the insult is the greater just because of the violation of a right. Often the victim of such behavior only makes things worse by demanding his rights, for he may thereby demonstrate his powerlessness. In fact, victims of such behavior sometimes adopt the strategy of not pressing their claims, as a means of ignoring and thereby (it is hoped) defusing or diminishing the insult. Undoubtedly there are, in addition to the above, other, often subtle, disadvantages to the recognition of rights. The point is simply that it's not transparently obvious that the ability to make claims is a good thing on the whole. It certainly isn't an unvarnished good, since it brings into existence new ways of getting hurt.

As a final point, we should note that there are societies in which people do not have the concept of a right, but in which people have dignity and self-respect. So there does not seem to be solid ground for believing that rights are essential for those goods, unless there is some special notion of, or part of, dignity and self-respect that are uniquely connected with the capacity for making claims on one's own behalf.

We have been looking at an argument supporting the value of rights. There is on the other hand a line of thought casting doubt on the importance and usefulness of the idea of a right. Rights are sometimes said to be the correlatives of duties. The idea is that wherever someone has a right, it is a right held against some other person, and the latter has a corresponding duty to the right-holder. On the strongest correlativity thesis, the converse is true also: wherever someone has a duty, it is owed to someone who has a corresponding right against the duty-holder. The relation is one of logic, distinguishing this correlativity thesis from the following two correlativity theses which are moral theses: (1) one who fails to fulfill certain of his duties forfeits certain of his rights (for example, a person who violates his duty not to harm others may forfeit his right to liberty, at least for a time); and (2) a being must have duties in order to have rights (this thesis has been used to deny that non-human animals can have rights).

The problem raised by the logical correlativity thesis is that if rights and duties are merely two sides of a coin—that is, if in all cases there is just a single relationship which can be looked at either from the side of the one who must do or refrain from doing something (the duty-holder), or from the side of the one to whom that performance is owed (the right-holder)—then rights are redundant in that we are talking about no more, when we talk about rights, than we were already talking about in talking of duties. Rights are just extra baggage, adding nothing to the moral enterprise. (This argument can be extended so that it applies not only to duties vis-a-vis rights, but also to disabilities vis-a-vis immunities and liabilities vis-a-vis powers.)

One might say: Well, at least rights-talk is as important as duty-talk in that we can regard duties as redundant and think entirely in terms of rights. This does not, however, seem intuitively plausible. Duties seem to be the indispensable items, perhaps because the language of duty has been around a lot longer, but more likely because in the end it is people's behavior that we are concerned with, and duties are more directly tied to what people are to do. There is, though, yet another argument for the indispensability of duties. The strongest correlativity thesis says that not only is there a corresponding duty wherever there is a right, but a corresponding right wherever there is a duty. The latter half of the thesis, however, turns out to be demonstrably false. (Feinberg, 1970, 244) Among one's duties is the duty of charity. A person's duty to give for charitable purposes can be fulfilled by giving to charities of his own choice, and (within limits) in amounts of his choosing. But there is no particular object of charity to which one owes anything; no potential object of charity can demand anything from a giver as its due. Thus, though there is a duty, there is no corresponding right. Another example is the supererogatory duty, or "ultra obligation." (Grice, 1967, ch. 4) Though we think of Albert Schweitzer's becoming a missionary doctor as an exemplary undertaking that was not morally required of him, he himself seems to have thought it his duty, and it seems true that there is a sense in which (given his ideals) even we can say that he had a duty. But of course we would not say that any of the beneficiaries of his mission had a right to it.

What we see, then, is that there are situations in which there are duties without corresponding rights. The language of duties is essential in characterizing these situations. So if it is a question whether it is duties or rights that are indispensable, duties so far get the nod—unless other cases can be found which argue for the indispensability of rights. This then remains a standing challenge for partisans of rights. For any theory of rights we may ask: is there a unique contribution being made by the notion of a right in this theory? Or are the rights in this theory merely echoes of other moral concepts which are the really significant ones. Are references to

rights merely summaries of other, more essential, moral information, or do they have independent moral standing, such that they
constitute the *basis* for ascribing duties (or whatever) to others?

Kinds and Characteristics of Rights

In discussions of rights it is not unusual to find a distinction between
liberties and what are called claim-rights. Some view this as a
distinction between two kinds of rights (or senses of 'rights'), while
others regard it as a distinction between rights and something else.
Whichever of these is the correct view of the matter, there is
undoubtedly a distinction of importance here, and there is much to
be said in elucidating it. In explaining the distinction I will refer to
liberties as rights, but will quickly take up the case for regarding
them as rights.

The distinction between liberties and claim-rights is most easily
explained by an example. If I see some money lying on the ground, I
have a right (am at liberty) to pick it up and keep it, provided that its
ownership is unknown. You also have a right to pick it up, and if you
do so first, I have no right, absent your permission, to appropriate it,
and I have no right (claim-right) to your handing it over to me. If, by
contrast, I have loaned you money, then I have a right (claim-right)
to your giving me the amount due by the appointed time for
repayment. Naturally liberties and claim-rights are not mutually
exclusive; if you owe me money, I have a right (claim-right) to your
repaying me, and also a right (liberty) to accept money tendered as
payment.

Claim-rights are often eludicated in terms of the duties of others;
they are paradigms for the correlativity thesis. If A has a right that B
repay borrowed money, then B has a duty to repay the money, and
conversely. Rights and duties are said to be correlative, and having a
right of this sort is often said to amount to someone else's owing a
duty to the rightholder. A liberty, by contrast, is sometimes explained as being simply the absence of a duty—more precisely, the
absence of a duty *not* to do something. If A is at liberty to pick up lost
money lying in the street, then he has no duty not to pick it up, and
conversely. But some writers have said that having a right to do
something involves more than the mere absence of a contrary duty;
they say that for a mere liberty to constitute a right, it must have a
claim aspect—that is, it must be connected in some way with the
duties of others. More precisely, it is said either that the liberty to do
x is either identical with or entails the duty of others not to interfere
(i.e., is either identical with or entails the (claim-) right not to be

interfered with by others), or else that, though the liberty to do x doesn't entail, it is entailed by, the right not to be interfered with. Both of these seem mistaken.

The following is a very nice example, from the legal scholar Wesley Newcomb Hohfeld, showing that liberties do not entail duties not to interfere:

A, B, C, and D, being the owners of [some] salad, might say to X: "Eat the salad, if you can; you have our license to do so, but we don't agree not to interefere with you." In such a case the privileges [i.e., liberty] exist, so that if X succeeds in eating the salad, he has violated no rights of any of the parties. But it is equally clear that if A had succeeded in holding so fast to the dish that X couldn't eat the contents, no right of X would have been violated. (Hohfeld, 1919, 41)

Furthermore, unless the notion of interference is restricted unduly, ordinary competition, such as for commercial markets, involves liberties but not the right not to be interfered with. It will not do to suggest that having a liberty entails having the right not to be interfered with in certain ways, such as assault, intimidation, or force, for these would be wrong even if one did not have whatever liberty is in question, and it would hardly be an explanation or defense of, say, my liberty to get drunk in my own house to point out that I have a right not to have my liquor stolen and a right not to be assaulted while imbibing.

Neither does the right not to be interfered with in doing x entail the liberty to do x. It may be illegal for private citizens to interfere with private gambling, but that does not mean that private gambling is permitted. And in a game such as football it may be illegal to interfere with an opponent in certain circumstances even though the opponent is not permitted to be where he is or to be doing what he is doing. Even those who violate rules are often accorded protection.

Some writers, agreeing with this distinction, hold that nevertheless the *right* to do x is different from the mere liberty to do x, and entails the right not to be interfered with. But consider my right to get drunk in my own house. Suppose my wife hides the liquor. Does she violate my right, or not? Remember that we are assuming that the right in question is more than a liberty. It follows that if I really have that right, then my wife violates it, and that if we say that she doesn't violate it, then I don't have the right at all. Both of these consequences are mistaken: I do have a right to get drunk in my own house, and my wife doesn't violate it in hiding the liquor. So we should reject the idea that a right has to be more than a mere liberty.

My right to get drunk in my own house is a liberty, though of course it will usually be accompanied by an additional right—the right not to be interfered with.

One reason that some believe a (mere) liberty can't or shouldn't be thought of as a right is that it isn't something that one can stand on in a demanding, confident way: "A right is something a man can *stand* on, something that can be demanded or insisted upon without embarrassment or shame." (Feinberg, 1973, 58) But while liberties can't be demanded in the same way that something that is owed can be demanded, one can certainly stand on his liberties in the sense that he can defend his behavior—loudly, insistently, urgently, and challengingly, if need be—by pointing to his liberty. One need not, in standing on his liberties, merely be excusing himself. So there is so far no compelling reason not to regard liberties as rights.

Thus far we have distinguished (a) N has a right to do x, from (b) N has a right not to be interfered with in doing x. These are distinct rights, even though they often occur together; indeed, many liberties would not be worth much if there were not also an accompanying right not to be interfered with that serves as a kind of protection for the liberty. It is important to be clear about the distinction between (a) and (b) because a theory of rights must be capable of dealing with the variety of kinds of rights that there are, and there are in addition two further classes of rights-assertions, possibly involving yet different kinds of rights, to consider. The first can be represented by the formula (c) N has a right to M's doing (or not doing) x. This is the typical formula for expressing a claim-right, and is the most obvious candidate for a logical correlation between one person's right and another's duty. The right not to be interfered with ((b), above) is construable as a case of (c): N's right not to be interfered with in doing x can be expressed as N's right to M's (i.e., others') not doing anything that would interfere with N's doing x.

The last kind of rights-assertion to be considered is represented by the formula (d) N has a right to x, where what is intended is not that N has a right to some designatable person or other acting (or not acting) in a certain manner, but that there is some thing or state of affairs to which N has a right, even if there is no one (though perhaps there ought to be) who presently owes him anything in connection with x. In this class are rights, asserted by some and denied by others, to adequate nutrition, to an education, to a means of livelihood, and others—the rights that are sometimes called social and economic rights. These rights-assertions differ from (c)-type rights-assertions in that in the (c)-type cases it is asserted that either everyone, or else some designatable individuals, owe a certain mode of behavior to the rightholder, whereas in the (d)-type cases, that to which the rightholder has a right may not (yet) be owed by other designatable individuals. Such rights are often asserted as a basis for arguing that there ought to be some sort of restructuring of social institutions, perhaps merely the creation of a special office, which will bring it about that people get what they have a right to.

There are, then, three different kinds of rights-assertions—(a), (c), and (d)—which must be kept in mind in trying to give a general theory of rights, though in the end perhaps not all of them can be defended as expressing genuine kinds of rights. Many theories of rights emphasize one kind of rights-assertion to the exclusion of others. What is needed is a unified account of rights, one that accounts for all conceptually legitimate rights-assertions. An adequate account must explain why different kinds of rights-assertions are properly assertions of *rights*. It is important, however, to note that not all the rights that people claim fit neatly into these categories, for some of them are rights-*packages*, or collections of the kinds of rights distinguished above. (Feinberg, 1973, 70) For example, the right to property is a rights-package consisting of, among others, the right (liberty) to enter the property (in the case of real property) and the right (claim-right) to others not entering without permission. One of the rights in the property package is the right to possess, which is itself a rights-package consisting of the right (liberty) to have physical control of a thing and the right (claim-right) to others not exercising control over it without permission. Thus, the full set of rights in the property rights package is rather large; *the* right to property is really many, usually separable, rights connected with property.

Absolute or Prima Facie

A perennial question regarding rights is whether they are absolute or prima facie. An absolute right is one that can't be overridden, by competing rights or other sorts of considerations, regardless of the circumstances.* A prima facie right is one that can thus be overridden, though it prevails in the absence of anything overriding it. The idea of a prima facie right will be discussed at greater length in chapter 3. At this point only a few matters will be discussed.

Not surprisingly, few writers think there are many absolute rights, if there are any at all, and some of the rights that are claimed to be absolute are so broad, abstract, and vague that it may not be clear exactly what more particular rights fall under their umbrellas.

---

*For other conceptions of absolute rights see Feinberg, 1978, 97-103 and references therein.

Furthermore, some writers who think that there are some absolute rights balk at regarding those rights as holding in extreme cases. For example, Robert Nozick regards rights as "side constraints," limitations on what it is permissible to do in seeking to attain one's ends. But Nozick explicitly leaves unanswered the question of whether side constraints are absolute, or whether they may be violated to avoid "catastrophic moral horror." (Nozick, 1974, 29-30) And Charles Fried says that moral rights are absolute, but that "we can imagine extreme cases where killing an innocent person may save a whole nation. In such cases it seems fanatical to maintain the absoluteness of the judgment. . . . And so the catastrophic may cause the absoluteness . . . to yield. . . ." (Fried, 1978, 10) Perhaps what is needed is a broad conception of ordinary morality, in which the usual moral notions apply with full force, and then a rather different moral framework for the extreme case. But it is extremely difficult to determine when we are faced with an extreme case, and there is no morally neutral way to do it.

Catastrophe occupies one end of a spectrum at the other end of which are matters we regard as trivial. If there are absolute rights, that may or may not apply in catastrophic situations, do they apply in trivial cases? There is, Fried says, an absolute right not to be intentionally caused physical harm. But though pinching causes some physical harm, because it is so trivial it does not have the same "moral quality" as killing, and there is no absolute right not to be pinched. (Fried, 1978, 30-31) This does not mean that it's all right to pinch someone for the fun of it. What it does mean is, that unlike killing, pinching enters into the calculus of utilities, so that a pinch is justified only if it will maximize utility and violate no absolute rights. Many white lies and lying social promises would also seem to fall into the category of the trivial, and so to be matters for utility calculations rather than rights.

Most people, I would guess, even if they think that some rights are absolute, think that absolute prohibitions don't apply in trivial cases. But if they don't apply, then there is the very difficult problem of distinguishing in a principled way between the cases in which absolute rights apply and the cases in which they don't. Inevitably, triviality will be taken to be a matter of the severity of the consequences of doing the acts in question—though only the consequences for those adversely affected may be considered, for if the consequences for those advantageously affected are also considered, many very serious acts will count as trivial, and the idea of absolute rights will be undermined.* Sometimes it is suggested that

*This point was brought to my attention by Mr. Christopher Hughes.

rights exist only if enough is at stake to warrant legal protection. This is not a satisfactory idea, for whether there should be legal protection depends on the costs of providing it, and the costs can change over time. That would mean that whether one has a right would depend in part on the costs of enforcement, and that rights can thus come and go, depending on the cost of a police force, courts, jails, etc. Further, this has the consequence that the more one needs the protection, the weaker the case for having a right, and the less one needs it, the stronger the case.

However we go about identifying the trivial, there is still the question of why the weighing of utilities is appropriate when the impacts on people are very great (the catastrophic cases) or very small (the trivial cases), but not when they are neither very great nor very small. Thus, the attempt to make the idea of absolute rights more palatable, by showing it to be in accord with most people's intuitions about catastrophic and trivial cases, threatens to under-mine it, at least until an explanation is forthcoming of why rights can't give way in the broad mid-range of cases. Here is one possible explanation: Rights might be conceived of as protecting some essential elements of personhood, such that there is no need for rights where personhood is not threatened. The application of this to trivial cases is obvious enough. For catastrophic cases the idea might be that personhood for social beings has a reality only within a minimally settled framework of social life. Thus, catastrophe could be understood as a situation seriously (i.e. imminently) threatening that framework, such that the recognition of absolute rights would undermine what it is supposed to protect. This is a possible line of thought for someone defending absolute rights as they are being understood here. It is not, though, the line of thought to be developed in this book.

Theories of Rights

The kinds of theories of rights to be discussed here are analytical in nature. They are theories not about what rights people have, but about what rights are, or what people have got when they have rights. Theories of the former sort will be discussed later.

Will theory

One of the most noteworthy proponents of this kind of theory is H. L. A. Hart. (Hart, 1955) Hart spelled the theory out for legal rights, but it seems to be extendable to moral rights as well. The idea is that to have a right is to stand in such a relation to another person that one can make a choice that controls the other's conduct. The one having the right is a small-scale sovereign with respect to the other: the right-holder expresses his will (within the scope of his authorization) and the other must behave accordingly. If, for example, we have agreed that I am to perform certain services for you in exchange for payment, and I have performed and want to be paid, then you must pay. I could, if I wish, waive your obligation to pay, or I can demand payment, and if you don't pay I have the choice whether to sue you or not. My having a right consists in my having these choices, which are powers the exercise of which alters your legal (and moral) situation. Hart suggests the model of a chain between two individuals, where the chain does not bind both of them, but only one, "the other end of the chain lying in the hands of another to use if he chooses." (Hart, 1955, 181)

There are several consequences that follow from this idea of what rights are, some of which may seem acceptable and others of which may not. For one thing, it follows from this view that animals and babies can't have rights since they lack the capacity for choice. It has been suggested that the relevant choices can be exercised by proxy (for example, by a guardian). But whereas an ordinary right-holder may, if he wishes, exercise his rights to his disadvantage as well as to his advantage, a guardian may not. So what seems central in the rights of animals (if they have any) and babies is not a choice that is respected, but the promotion or protection of interests.

Another consequence of Hart's view, in its application to law, is that it applies mainly to civil law, for in areas such as torts and contracts an individual does have choices to make which the law will respect. There are also some welfare functions of the state where choice is noteworthy, for it's up to an eligible individual whether or not to demand benefits. But in the criminal law, on this view, there are no rights. There is, for example no right not to be harmed, for it's usually not up to the individual whether to allow the harm (by consenting), or whether to prosecute, since prosecuting powers belong to officials and the individual harmed can only complain to them, which is no guarantee that they will prosecute. This point was made some time ago by John Chipman Gray in *The Nature and Sources of the Law*:

The legal rights of a man are the rights which are exercisable on his motion. A man has, therefore, no legal rights as to those interests in the realizing of which he is protected only by other people exercising their rights. The fact that the State can punish the burglar who breaks into my house does not give *me* any right not to have my house broken into. (Gray, 1921, 19)

Even by Hart's own reckoning, rights-as-legally-respected-choices needs to be supplemented by other conceptions. Constitutional (fundamental) rights are rights which limit the power of a legislature to make law; they are immunities, protecting us from certain adverse legal changes. And yet another notion of rights is involved in the criticism of law—a notion in terms of which we *can* talk of people having rights (to life and personal security) that are protected by laws against murder and assault.

Hart himself accepts all of the above consequences, though it is open to anyone to try to press them as criticisms. There are further consequences, though, which are harder to swallow. Consider those rights, like the right to education in our country or the right to vote in some other countries, which are said not only to be rights but to be duties as well. If one has a duty to be educated, then one has no choice, and so on Hart's view has no right to be educated. The point is, as it was with the rights of animals and babies, that it is the benefit, not the choice, that seems to take first place in the right to an education. Related to this are cases of apparent rights that one is not allowed to waive. People are said to have a right not to be enslaved, but they are not permitted to waive this right. Likewise one usually cannot consent to being beaten (i.e., cannot waive the right not to be beaten). And under current occupational safety laws an employee can't waive his right to work in a safe environment. On Hart's view none of these turn out to be rights. Indeed, there is an interesting irony here. Rights are thought of as protecting us, but as the protection increases as in the above cases, on the will theory the right disappears. (MacCormick, 1977, 195-199)

Rights as claims

This view, attributable to Joel Feinberg, has certain features in common with the foregoing view, but its basic idea is different. The simple statement of the view is that rights are valid claims, but in order to grasp the idea the complex practice of claiming must be explained. The central notion is "making claim to" something. First, an example that will serve as a model. Under the rules governing gaining title to land, a person may qualify for a title. He then "has a claim" to a given piece of land. To take possession he presents his title, thereby "making claim to" the land. The latter is the performative sense of claiming, for the act of "making claim to" is an act having legal consequences: it makes something happen, legally speaking.

The analogy to the moral case is this. Certain principles may give a person a claim (make it the case that one "has a claim"). One presents his claim, not in the form of a chit or a title, but in the form of an argument, and if it outweighs other claims, one is in a position to "make claim to" certain behavior on the part of another person. It is at the stage that the claim withstands challenges, such that one may "make claim to" another's behavior, that one's claim is valid, and one can be said to have a right.

There is much that is plausible in this, though the elements with which I agree will not become clear until chapter 3. There are, however, some of the same difficulties that arose for the will theory. One of these is the problem of unwaivable rights (Feinberg calls them "mandatory" rights) such as the right to education. For according to Feinberg the claim that one has when he is in a position to "make claim to" certain conduct by another is one with respect to which he has discretion. (Feinberg, 1977, 33) It is up to him whether to press his valid claim. But when a right is also a duty, there is no discretion, for there is only a "half-liberty"—liberty to go to school or to be vaccinated, but no liberty not to go to school or not to be vaccinated. Feinberg's answer is that these are not really rights at all.

. . . the rights in question are best understood as ordinary duties with associated half-liberties rather than ordinary claim-rights with associated full liberties, but . . . the performance of the duty is presumed to be so beneficial to the person whose duty it is that he can *claim* the necessary means from the state and noninterference from others as *his* due. Its character as claim is precisely what his half-liberty shares with the more usual (discretionary) rights and what warrants his use of the word 'right' in demanding it. (Feinberg, 1977, 34)

Feinberg seems to have incorporated an element of interest or benefit theory here—that having a right is a matter of there being an important interest at stake.

Feinberg's account treats claim-rights as exhaustive of rights. But there is, of course, the question, discussed earlier, of whether liberties can be rights, and there are other sorts of rights—powers and immunities—which Feinberg's account would have to be modified to accomodate.

Finally, Feinberg recognizes one significant qualification of his view. On his account all rights are claims *to* some good and *against* someone. But he recognizes as legitimate what he calls "a special 'manifesto sense' of 'right,' in which a right need not be correlated with another's duty." (Feinberg, 1970, 225) A poor and starving person has a great need, and thus has a claim for food "against the world, even if against no one in particular." (Feinberg, 1970, 225) This person has a claim that is not at present valid because there is no one on whom a corresponding duty can be imposed. Yet Feinberg acquiesces in regarding such "potential rights" as "determinants of *present* aspirations and guides to *present* policies." (Feinberg, 1970, 255) Again, a concession to some sort of interest theory.

Rights as entitlements

The most recent difficulties are avoided on the account of rights as entitlements, espoused by H. J. McCloskey. (McCloskey, 1965) Rights on this view are rights *to* some good but not rights *against* anyone. Of course, rights do usually give rise to duties of others, but something can be a right that does not do so. Thus, what Feinberg calls rights in a special "manifesto sense" but not in the full sense, are rights in the full sense according to McCloskey.

It is part of McCloskey's conception, in light of the foregoing, that the substance of rights derives entirely from the character of human beings and their needs, and not from their relations at a given time with other people. For rights understood in terms of a set of duties against certain individuals are in a continually changing state. But, to the contrary, we do, and correctly, talk of a fixed, stable set of rights that people have.

It is often objected to the rights-as-entitlements view that the notion of an entitlement is hardly clearer than the notion of a right, and so does not do much if anything to illuminate the latter. To the extent that I understand the notion of an entitlement, however, it seems too strong for explaining rights, at least as McCloskey sees them. For by my linguistic sense the notion of entitlement seems a rather conclusive notion. When one is entitled to something, the title to it hardly seems overridable—the winner of the race is entitled to first prize, and other considerations are irrelevant in awarding it. But rights, as McCloskey conceives of them, can come into conflict and can be outweighed on occasion.

This highlights a significant difference between McCloskey and Feinberg. McCloskey regards rights as items that are different from and capable of supporting the imposing of duties on people, whereas Feinberg seems to regard rights as the valid impositions of duties on others, and what backs these up, according to Feinberg, are not items called rights, but the claims that one has, which are derived from general moral principles. For McCloskey, then, as I read him (though he is not entirely clear about this), the central case is what is sometimes called a general right (e.g., the right to free speech, or the right to a minimum income), which can be overridden on some occasions, whereas for Feinberg it is a special right, which is a right one has on a particular occasion against some specific individual. The general-special distinction is an important one—indeed, a number of such distinctions have been made. This will be taken up in Chapter 3.

Benefit theory

The idea behind this theory is that what is essential in rights is the protection or promotion of people's interests. In particular, having a right means being the beneficiary of a duty. Historically this has been a popular theory of legal rights because the idea that rights are created by imposing duties on others fits neatly into positivistic theories of law. According to classical legal positivism laws are commands from the lawmaker to the citizen, and to have a duty is simply to be the addressee of a command of the sovereign. Rights can't be part of law unless they can be related to commands, and so it is natural to regard the having of a right as being just the beneficiary of a duty. Bentham's version of the theory was simply that to have a right is to stand to benefit from a duty, but it is easy to show that as it stands that is inadequate. If I tell you that I will give you a book that you want when Jones returns it to me, then you stand to benefit from Jones's fulfilling his duty, and on Bentham's view this means you have a right to Jones's returning it. But of course you don't.

This theory has been improved upon in a version called the qualified beneficiary theory. (Lyons, 1969, 176) To have a right is to be the "direct, intended beneficiary" of a duty. This version avoids the problem raised above for the unqualified version, for you are neither the direct nor the intended beneficiary of Jones's duty to return my book. Notice also that this theory deals with a problem that arose in connection with Hart's theory that rights are legally recognized choices, namely, the problem of how there can be rights under the criminal law since the beneficiaries of those laws have no choice in the matter. In the present theory ordinary citizens have rights under the criminal law just by being the direct, intended beneficiaries of the duties they impose.*

One problem case that has been raised concerns the third party beneficiary. Suppose I promise you that I will look after your Aunt while you are gone. Your Aunt, a third party to the promise, is the direct, intended beneficiary, but not being a party to the promise she has no right to my performance. You, being the promisee, do have a right to it, but you are not the direct, intended beneficiary.

*There may, however, be other laws that raise similar problems for the qualified beneficiary theory. See Lyons, 1969, 184-185.

David Lyons has answered (Lyons, 1969, 180-184) that the third party beneficiary does have a right to the performance—not only in morals, but even sometimes in law: the point is confirmed by noting that the Aunt can waive the benefits if she wishes. And you too are a direct intended beneficiary, in that you want the promise kept, and my keeping it is thus intended as a good to you and accrues directly to you.

There are, though, two additional doubts about the benefit theory, both connected with the correlativity thesis. First, if there are, in law, rights that do not (always, anyway) correlate with duties, then the theory is in error. And there do seem to be rights of this sort. One can have an easement over land which, at the moment, has no owner, and so it does not seem plausible to construe the easement-rights as the benefits that are to accrue from someone else's observance of his duties. And MacCormick gives as an example the right (in Scotland) of the children of an intestate to be given ownership of the intestate's property by the executor of the estate. This cannot, he says, be construed as an ordinary right-duty relationship because the right exists even prior to the appointment of the executor, and what is more, the very identity of the right-holder influences the appointment of the executor. (MacCormick, 1977, 200-201)

The second problem for the benefit theory is simply the one raised earlier with respect to the correlativity thesis—that rights seem to be dispensable if they are just the concomitants, or 'reflexes', of duties.

2

Utilitarianism and Rights

Utilitarianism is a substantive theory in morals, law, and politics. It regards the maximization of human welfare (leaving other sentient creatures aside for the purposes of this discussion) as the touchstone of permitted or required behavior. But though all utilitarians agree on this touchstone, there are different ideas about how exactly it yields norms regulating behavior, and as a result there are different ideas not only about what substantive norms, but also about what kinds of norms, it yields. All utilitarian theories embrace moral duties as among these norms, but according to some utilitarians human welfare also grounds rights.

Non-utilitarian rights-theorists object on two fronts to utilitarians who propound theories of rights. On the one hand they claim that utilitarianism does not capture all of the rights that an adequate theory of rights should capture. On the other hand objectors claim that utilitarians, by virtue of their views about the nature of rights, cannot give an adequate account of the ways in which rights function in moral deliberation and argument. I am in agreement with the critics. It seems to me that there are unanswered difficulties both with utilitarianism's analytic and its substantive claims about rights. These problems will be developed in this chapter.

The Entrenchment of Rules

(1) Many utilitarians who think there are rights subscribe to some variation of Mill's account (Mill, 1959) in explaining how human welfare supports rights. The theme is as follows: There are certain aspects of human welfare and well-being (for example, life and

20

health) that are particularly important and peculiarly vulnerable. Due in large part to people's inability to calculate correctly which of their actions would really maximize human good, we would on the whole be better off if these aspects of welfare and well-being were protected by imposing sanctions for injuring or threatening injury to people. This can be done in one or more of three ways—by creating legal proscriptions and legal sanctions; by getting society at large to accept certain ways of behaving, and to impose informal sanctions for deviations or threatened deviations; and/or by training people, particularly when they are young, to think and behave in certain ways and to feel guilt when they fail to do so, or when they even think of doing so. The basic theme, then is the *entrenchment of certain rules*, formally in overt institutions, and informally in accepted modes of behavior. There are various reasons, according to utilitarians, for entrenching these rules. They involve aspects of welfare and well-being that are important and vulnerable, their vulnerability owing to the interests others have in disregarding them. Even if, it is thought, people are genuinely determined to pursue the general welfare and not (or not just) their own welfare, it is so easy to miscalculate, and so hard to avoid preferring oneself, that some form of institutionalization is necessary. For if people were, in the ways mentioned above, prevented from directly pursuing overall welfare and well-being, human good would, it is argued, be maximized. We would collectively be better off if people, even in their attempts to make things better, were to keep hands off those aspects of human good.

There are further reasons given by some utilitarians (or, more generally, consequentialists) for entrenchment of certain rules. One is what is called the coordination problem. Often it happens that a person is faced with a situation in which the act that it would be best (promote the greatest good) to do depends on what someone else is going to do. It might be best for me to do A if you are going to do B, but to do C if you are going to do D, but I must make my decision not knowing what you will do. Of course, this occurs not only where there are only two people involved, but where there are many, and the problem is that the outcome that is best for everyone is not likely to be realized if each person must decide how to act in ignorance of how others will act. Entrenching rules provides a way of realizing, even if not perfectly, the desired outcome. There is, besides this, yet another reason for entrenching rules. Thus far we have considered contributions to human welfare which derive, as it were, from the "objects", such as health, of certain actions and policies. But in the distribution of these goods there is in addition another good that is "parasitic" on the first. People can derive benefits not only from what they finally get in a distribution, but from control over, or power in the making of, the distribution. Thus Thomas Scanlon says that among the goods available to people are "forms of discretion over which individuals are in conflict," (Scanlon, 1978, 102) and holds that "the case for rights derives in large part from the goal of promoting an acceptable distribution of control over important factors in our lives." (Scanlon, 1978, 103) This line of thought is said to support rules assigning, among others, freedom of expression and rights of privacy, for there is value not only in achieving the best outcomes, but also in being able to make our own choices and in others recognizing our being entitled to make them.

Now what, as utilitarians see it, does the fact that certain utility-maximizing rules (or in general, rules designed to promote any sorts of ends) should be entrenched have to do with rights? How does this fact, or even the actual entrenchment of rules, yield rights? What is the form of the transition from "This rule exists (or should exist)" to "I have a right"? One possibility is that a person might be said to have a right in the sense that there is a rule that entitles him to something. Think for example of a game such as Monopoly. There is a rule in that game saying that the salary for passing Go is $200. Given that rule, a player has a right to be given $200 when he passes Go. Even if there is no rule of that sort, there might be other rules from which it could be inferred that there is a right to $200 on passing Go. There is also another way in which rights might get into the picture. Rather than infer rights from rules, we might have rules that explicitly confer rights. The rule in Monopoly might say that one who passes Go has a right to $200. Similarly in law: A statute might say that when a debtor dies, certain creditors have a right to certain of the debtor's property; but even if no right is explicitly conferred, there may be statutes from which such a right can be inferred. In either case what we have, in utilitarianism, is rights being created by the assignment of claims within an institution to various individuals.

Now rights of this sort can have little, if any, role in serious social criticism. Groups of people might justly complain that they are being deprived of their rights in that they are not getting what the rules entitle them to, but in that sense of having a right one cannot complain of the rules themselves. So if one is to be able to complain about social institutions themselves in the name of rights denied, rights must be derivable in the utilitarian framework in yet another way. One possibility is to say that if there is a utilitarian justification for the establishment of an institution (a set of institutional rules), then everyone (or at least those who would be benefited by it) has a right to its establishment. This is a plausible suggestion, and it provides an explanation of how rights might have a serious role in social criticism. This idea might even gain some support from a feature of it that some people think true of rights—that someone can have a right even if there is, at the moment, no one who has a duty to do anything about it.

But despite the foregoing, something does not ring true about the idea that there is a right where, and only where, there is a utilitarian justification for the establishment of institutional rules. There are costs—utilitarian losses—involved in institutionalizing rules. Not only might there be administrative costs and utilitarian losses in the imposition of sanctions, but there are also disutilities to those on whom the rules will work disadvantages. Now one problem is that costs can vary, with the result that at one time there may be a right and at another time not. Furthermore, one of the costs of institution-alizing something is the psychic distress that some may experience at the prospect of entrenching certain rules, with the result that whether one has a right will be determined in part by whether others like the idea. We might, of course, just rule out this disutility, but it's hard to see any grounds for this within utilitarianism. Or we might say that in the long run this distress will dissipate, as people get used to the new institutions; but the trouble with this is that it might be true of virtually anything—for example people can, after all, get used to very little privacy.

(2) Utilitarians are not clear as to whether, as they see it, all rights either exist within the framework of justified institutions or else are rights to the establishment of such institutions. It does seem, though, that there are rights apart from institutions and some utilitarians (perhaps not the same ones referred to above) have tried to give an account of them. The idea is that the principle of utility sometimes imposes duties directly on some individuals, and that at least where the duty is owed directly to and for the benefit of another individual, the latter has a right to the performance of the duty. This connection between duties and rights is called the correlativity thesis, or more precisely, the thesis of the logical correlativity of rights and duties. Now in its strongest form—that whenever there is a duty there is a correlative right, and *vice versa*—the correlativity thesis is not correct, as we have seen in chapter 1, for there are certain duties, such as the duty to give to charity, that have no correlative rights. But there are two aspects of the correlativity thesis that appear plausible and are required by this utilitarian attempt to account for extra-institutional rights. First, it must be the case that wherever there is such a right, someone else has a duty to the right-holder, and second, that the existence of that

right can be derived from the existence of the duty. For utilitarianism is basically a theory of obligation, and if there are non-institutional rights, they can't exist independent of others' duties, and can be known only by being derived from these duties.

However, neither of these features of correlativity required by a utilitarian account of rights holds up. For one thing, there appear to be cases where a person could have a right even though no one else has a related duty to him. Suppose Jones and Smith enter into a contract. Smith performs his part of the contract, but Jones dies before doing his part. It seems to me that it could happen that there is, at least for a time, no one who has a duty to Smith, and no rule by which to determine who owes a duty, and yet I think that Smith would still have rights under the contract—rights which would form a basis for *imposing* duties on others. Again, suppose I have an easement over your property, and then you cease to own the property, and, at least for a time, no one owns it. I think I still have, or could have, a right to cross the property, a right that others do not have, though there is no one against whom I have this right. (See Benditt, 1978, 171-173) As a final example, it may be that certain American Indian claims might be understood as rights without (presently) correlative duties. I do not, however, regard these cases as presenting overwhelming objections to a utilitarian account of non-institutional rights. One could, I suppose, give up the intuitions supporting the cases I have described, though one would also have to have a different idea than we are often inclined to have as to the reason why someone else comes to have a duty to the rightholder.

But there is a more difficult problem, which concerns liberties, or permissions. To have a liberty is, at the least, to be permitted to do something—i.e., one has a liberty (or is at liberty to do something) when his doing something is not prohibited. Are liberties rights? If they are, they must, on utilitarianism, be construed as correlatives of duties—in particular, the duty not to interfere. In other words, liberties must be understood to be rights not to be interfered with in certain ways. This means that having a right not to be interfered with in a certain way is equivalent to, or entails, an entitlement to behave in a given way. However, this equivalence or entailment does not exist. You might have a duty not to interfere with me in any way in connection with some money that you have dropped and I have picked up and pocketed, but that does not mean that I may keep the money. Again, I may have no right to (a duty not to) interfere in any way with your gambling, but that does not mean that you are allowed to gamble. In general, then, being permitted to do something is not the same as, nor is it entailed by, having a right not to be interfered with in doing it, though a liberty without that right might not be very secure (morally speaking).

Some writers say that (bare) liberties are not rights; rather, they say, to have a right is to have *both* a liberty and a claim (a right not to be interfered with). Whatever the merits of this idea on its own terms (see chapter 1), it will not help a utilitarian, for on utilitarianism non-institutional rights must be derived from others' duties, and a right understood as both a liberty and a claim cannot be derived merely from a duty not to interfere, nor from that together with other duties. In any event, even if liberties without claims are not rights, they can exist, and a utilitarian must be able to account for them. And the problem is that, for a utilitarian, anything that is normative or prescriptive but non-institutional can be derived only from duties. So if bare liberties can't be derived from duties, utilitarianism can't account for them.

(3) Let us return to the versions of utilitarianism that find rights imbedded in social institutions that themselves have utilitarian backing. Critics have plagued utilitarians with the question of why anyone would follow the rules when it is apparent that violating them, on some occasions, would promote more good than following them. Utilitarians have rightly reminded us, of course, that indirect utilities must also be counted—including the impact on the institution itself of the violation, and the impact on people's proclivities to rule-following generally, particularly the violator's own proclivities. Nevertheless it has seemed to critics that even when all of this is considered, violating a rule on some occasion might be best.

John Rawls suggested in "Two Concepts of Rules" (Rawls, 1955) that we think in terms of different roles or offices. There is the role of legislator, and the role of judge, or rule-applier. The legislator is to think in utilitarian terms—he is to establish rules the acceptance of which will promote the greatest good. But the judge's office precludes him from considering the case before him in utilitarian terms; he must think about it only in terms of the rules. There are, indeed, a number of areas in which a distinction is often made between the morality of a role and the morality of individual decisions made by those occupying the roles. For example, the lawyer's role is often said to include, and justifiably so, zealous representation, the assertion of technical defenses, and confidentiality, with the result that lawyers have only to act as the role prescribes and make no (or few) moral choices involving these matters. This, it is thought, avoids the objection that there are occasions when violating a rule would be for the best, for in a rule-applying context one never has to consider violating a rule on the ground that it would be better to do so.

This suggestion has not seemed very satisfactory. It is understandable that the role of judge should preclude the individual who fills it from appealing directly to utilitarian considerations, but it is not clear why a real judge, who is a person, should forget about the principle of utility. And it is even less clear why any ordinary individual should, in making moral assessments, forget about the principle of utility itself and instead think in terms of the roles of moral law-maker and moral law-applier. And even if one does this, it is not clear why this utilitarian law-maker and law-applier should stick to his rules when it is plain to him that it is not for the best. One could, of course, just insist that this is what people should do, but this has never seemed convincing.

Now we must not tax utilitarians too much here. There is a criticism of utilitarianism which says that in order for rights to have real moral force, one must be allowed to look only at the right involved when there is a violation, and must never look at the utilities. So, it is said, if utilitarianism is to give us an adequate account of rights, it must not permit a utilitarian legislator or anyone else to look directly at the utilities in making a moral assessment of an actual situation. For to do so is to fail to give rights the moral force that they really have. One cannot have a genuine obligation to adhere to a rule unless one is barred from directly considering the ultimate values grounding the rule, and inasmuch as utilitarianism does not prohibit this, it can't give an adequate theory of rights. (Lyons, 1980)

This seems too strong. I take it to be a feature of rights, and one to which not enough attention has been paid, that a person can have a right that he ought not to exercise, and similarly that one might have a right to another person's behaving in a certain way, that the right-holder ought not to insist upon. So even though one might be fully justified in exercising or insisting on his right, even without examining the utilities to determine whether he ought to do so, nevertheless one is not precluded by his right from doing so. And if it is all right for a right-holder to look at the utilities to determine whether he should exercise or insist on his right, then it is surely all right for others to do so, for the purpose of suggesting to the right-holder that he ought not to exercise or insist on his right. In short, bringing rights into the picture does not entirely take utilities out of the picture, and it is a mistake to think that a theory of rights is defective in permitting one to look beyond rights to utilities.

Let us return to the main line of thought in this section, which concerns the question of why, if at all, a utilitarian would insist on following a right-conferring rule when violating the rule would promote greater good. A possible answer is as follows. First of all, it is possible to be mistaken about whether violating a rule will be better than following it, and if one allows himself the liberty of looking directly at the utilities, he is likely to make some mistakes. Further, if others see you ignoring rules in favor of utilities when *you* think it better to violate the rules, they might be encouraged to do so when *they* think it better to violate rules, and in the end many mistakes are likely to be made. So it would be better, all in all, if people were to make it a rule never to decide cases by direct appeal to utilities. Of course, this means that in particular cases one will not be wholeheartedly behind the social rule in question, for one will believe, on the merits (the utilities) of the case that the rule should be violated, but will advocate compliance, and hence will advocate something that he does not believe.

In the best of all utilitarian worlds (given the human limitations that make it best from a utilitarian point of view to institutionalize social rules), one will genuinely believe in the moral ideas he advocates, for there will be lost utilities when people fail to do so, not the least of which will result from the tendency to backslide by one who advocates what he does not believe. So a utilitarian, to forestall this, should try to come to believe in what he advocates— namely, the rules whose entrenchment promotes the greatest good. This achieved, there is no longer any serious problem for utilitarians due to the fact that sometimes violating a rule would be best.

This is about as far as utilitarians can go in trying to deal with the problem. But even if it's possible for a person to wean himself from thinking too much, or too often, about his ultimate moral concern, there still seems to be something quite paradoxical in it. Let us suppose that someone has weaned himself thoroughly, so that his advocacy of the rules is uncontaminated by his (supposed) ultimate moral concern. At this point he has got himself into a position where it is no longer open to him to re-evaluate the rules to see if they still promote the greatest good. Now I take it that no utilitarian can accept this. It may be, though, that this is not a possible state of affairs, but even if it is not, it indicates a limit to the utilitarian argument. For the possibility of revising the rules requires people continually to look at the utilities served by the rules, and this must inevitably lead them to ask why they should stick with the rules when violating them is best.

On utilitarianism, as on any instrumental theory of rights, there is a lack of congruity between rights (understood as institutional rules) and the ultimate ends they serve. This lack of congruity shows up at the level of justification, when the question is whether to follow the rule or not, and it also shows up when the question is what one should advocate. Advocating the rule might yield greater success in promoting the ultimate end, but a utilitarian is then stuck with an incongruity between what he thinks and what he says, and avoiding the incongruity might damage the ultimate end. I am inclined to regard this as a serious defect, on the ground that a moral theory cannot live with a false face. It seems to me that it should be a condition of adequacy for a moral theory that advocating it is not barred by the theory itself, and that it should not be capable of producing a division in society between the manipulators, who advocate views they both don't fully accept and have no reason always to follow, and the gulls, who think that the rules being advocated are to be accepted at face value.

Utilitarian Rights

(4) What rights do people have, according to utilitarians? Despite the fact that according to utilitarians rights are a function of what rules would promote the greatest good, and that calculations of human good are difficult at best, most utilitarians seem sure that utilitarianism supports the standard battery of liberal rights. And most of them seem confident that even if such rights were not already largely established in society, utilitarianism would support entrenching them. One feels, however, that utilitarians do not acquire their devotion to those rights by first determining what the utilities favor; and even if institutionalizing certain rules can be expected to promote average welfare, critics are inclined to doubt that that is the only reason to have them. My own view is along the lines of this last observation, for it seems to me that we are prepared to endorse certain rights even if we are in doubt as to the utilities. (It's not as if we endorse rights merely on the basis of giving them the benefit of any doubts we may have about the utilities—why do that?) Indeed, I think that we do endorse certain rights even though we are unclear about the utilities, and that we are prepared to hold onto these rights even if we were to become convinced that they diminish average welfare.

For one thing, as indicated earlier a person can have a right that he ought not to act on, or a right to another person's behavior that he ought not to insist on. Now the reason one sometimes ought not to act on, or insist on, a right is often that to do so would be worse (in terms of utilities) than not doing so. Notice that this fact does not, or at least need not, defeat the claim that there is a right. The problem being raised here is not that utilitarians cannot account for the fact that sometimes one ought not to insist on his rights—Mill, for example, holds that there are duties of beneficence that are distinct from duties of justice and hence from rights. The problem is rather that for utilitarians, rules that confer rights might not be institutionalizable unless we can predict that if they were to be institutionalized, people *would* fulfill their duties of beneficence—that is, that people wouldn't insist on their rights to the extent that things would be better if the rights didn't exist.

What I am supposing is this: that I have a right—for example, to ignore someone, or to say something that I want to say; that it would on the whole be more hurtful if I were to act on my right than if I were not to act on it; that I really ought not to act on my right; but that, inasmuch as I do have the right, I will be justified in acting on it. (See chapter 3.) Now what one might do, many might do, and it seems to me not impossible (to say the least) that on the whole average utility would be greater if people refrained from acting on and insisting on the rights that they admittedly have. In fact, it is hard to believe that the world (or at least our corner of it) would not be better, on average, if people did not insist so much on their rights—even the ones that utilitarians support. And even if this were not so at one time in our history, it is hard to believe that it would not be so at some time or other in our past or future.

But of course if that is ever so, then at least at that time a utilitarian would have to abjure his claim to have rights—unless, that is, there are other utilities that we have overlooked. Some utilitarians do, to be sure, hold that we must consider not only the effects of people's acts and failures to act, but also the benefits that accrue to rightholders merely from having the authority to decide for themselves how to act. There is great utility for individuals in being able to plan their lives, to experiment with ways of living, even if they sometimes make mistakes. And one aspect of this is the utility gained in being able to decide for oneself whether to act on, or insist on, a right, or to give way for the good of others even when one does not have to.

Now there is undoubtedly utility in having the authority to make these decisions oneself—there might even be additional utility in one's being able to feel charitable, or whatever, on the occasions when one does give way for the good of others. But the experience of mankind does not show, at least as this observer sees it, that these utilities inevitably offset the losses that are brought about by people insisting on their rights. In any event I should not like to see the case for rights rest on such a foundation as this. It seems to me that rights are not dependent for their existence on the good will of their possessors, and that there are rights even where we can predict that average utility will be lowered because of the extent to which people will exercise them in the face of the weightier interests of others.

(5) Even aside from questions about people acting on or insisting on their rights when it would be better if they didn't, there are questions to be raised about whether, apart from that, institutionalizing certain rules would really increase average utility. That is, there are questions about whether the battery of liberal rights widely favored by utilitarians are really supported by their theory.

Liberals recognize rights connected with personality—rights that are needed to enable people to develop and express their personalities, and perhaps even a right to self-development, self-realization, and the like. Utilitarian liberals favor such rights because they regard them as being productive of individual and social welfare, where utility derives both from the results achieved in the way of self development, and from the freedom to experiment and choose for oneself. Of course, not every form of self-realization is to be encouraged, for it can be positively harmful to self and others, and so for utilitarians advocacy of these rights rests in part on predictions as to the sorts of self-development people will undertake.

The pluralism that free self-development leads to is seen by some as itself desirable—even exhilarating. Yet it is hard sometimes not to see advantages to orthodoxy, even if only as a momentary palliative to occasional tension, fear, and doubt. Of course, orthodoxy purchased by overt repression is not so good, but there are more benign forms than that, and everyone must sometimes wonder whether that wouldn't be better. And Richard Taylor's example of an anti-religionist bent on upsetting the religious orientation of a tightknit, devout group of individuals raises another sort of question about pluralism. (Taylor, 1973)

Though some people want some sort of orthodoxy for themselves, many want to be free to go their own ways, to develop themselves the best they can, free from the fetters of social orthodoxy. And it is undoubtedly true that many people can make more of themselves, and be happier, if permitted to do this. But it is a fallacy, one with which liberals are often charged, to argue that because each individual would be better off if he or she were free to develop as they wish, it would be best to arrange social institutions so as to maximize opportunities for free self-development—just as it would be a mistake to argue that since each of us individually would be better off operating a car, the greatest good overall would be produced if social institutions were arranged so as to maximize opportunities for people to operate cars.

Well, then, does free self-development promote the greatest good overall? For my part, I would like to think that it does, though I often have doubts about it. But I never entertain similar doubts about whether there are rights with respect to self-development and self-realization. Often when there are choices to be made between an individual's having to be a certain sort of person for the benefit of society, and society having to make a lot of room for what some individuals want to be, it seems clear to me that the latter is correct. It seems clear to me, then, that my belief in rights of personality does not depend on any ideas about what's best on the whole. I think that such rights would exist even if it were not best on the whole that they exist, and that it is not justifiable to curtail such rights even at those times when there is actually reason to think that it is not for the best.

Similar points can be made regarding the right of privacy, which is a right that many utilitarian liberals advocate—though it should be mentioned that not even all non-utilitarian liberals think that there is such a right. Recently a rather different version of utilitarianism has been developed, particularly in connection with law. It is called economic analysis, and its adherents regard it as providing a very powerful tool both for understanding past legal developments and for providing grounds for future directions. Economic analysis starts from the assumptions that everything of value has a market price, and that in a perfect market—one in which all exchanges that people wish to make (given their levels of wealth) are made, and made costlessly (without costs of negotiation and the like)—everyone would eventually get to a position of not wishing any further exchanges. This could only be because no one would regard any further exchanges as bettering his position. So if in the real world people are still willing to make further exchanges, but are prevented from making them, then the situation is suboptimal from the standpoint of total wealth, so that things would on the whole (or, on the average) be better if such exchanges were facilitated.

One way to facilitate exchanges is by reducing the transaction costs, so that people will find it worthwhile to negotiate and exchange things of value. The lower the costs of transacting, the more transactions, and since in a voluntary transaction each party thinks himself better off, more transactions mean more total good, or wealth. Sometimes, however, there is no way to reduce transaction costs sufficiently to make it cost-effective for people to transact. In such cases, argue the economic theorists, the thing to do is to try to anticipate the market: determine what exchanges people would make but for the transaction costs, and then arrange social institutions so as to yield these outcomes.

This leads us to the role of law, though the argument is not limited entirely to law. As in morals, so in law, decisions must be made as to what rights to recognize. Economic analysts have noticed that the allocation of rights is one way, and a very significant one, of anticipating the market—that is, of producing outcomes that a market in things of value would produce if it were cost-effective for people to make exchanges. For example, suppose a company wants to build a factory whose operations will pollute the air. If we "give" to nearby residents a right not to have such a factory built, the company can build only if it purchases these rights from each individual. But the costs of negotiating all these agreements are so high that even if it would otherwise be profitable to buy the rights and build the factory, it will not be built. So assigning rights to the residents is inefficient, and the better course might be to give the company the right to build, but give residents the right to compensation if they are in fact damaged. If it would be profitable to build the factory even with this added expense, then it will be built, and efficiency is served. The point is that people are taken to have the rights it would be economically efficient for them to have, and for that reason alone.

A similar argument has been made with respect to rights of privacy. Richard Posner, one of the foremost economic analysts, argues that what is at stake here is control of information, which is necessary for the smooth functioning of a market. To the extent that exchanges are made on the basis of misinformation, they fail, on the whole, to increase utility, and to the extent that people are doubtful about their information, they waste resources trying to become informed and are hesitant about making exchanges, both of which are impediments to the smooth functioning of markets and hence to the maximizing of value. This is the economic argument against fraud in commerce—allowing sellers to misrepresent their goods is economically inefficient. "But," Posner argues,

people "sell" themselves as well as their goods. They profess high standards of behavior in order to induce others to engage in social or business dealings with them from which they derive an advantage but at the same time they conceal some of the facts that these acquaintances would find useful in forming an accurate picture of their character. (Posner, 1978, 399)

Therefore, Posner argues, "everyone should be allowed to protect himself from disadvantageous transactions by ferreting out concealed facts about individuals which are material to the representations (implicit or explicit) that those individuals make concerning their moral qualities." (Posner, 1978, 400) Posner finds powerful evidence that people wish to control information about themselves for the purpose of manipulating others in the fact that so many people are not naturally reticent, but rather are willing to divulge even discreditable information about themselves to complete strangers—i.e., in situations where friends, relatives, associates, etc. will not find out.

Undoubtedly there is much truth in what Posner says. Activities such as prying and eavesdropping have costs for their victims, but in hiding information the latter are often attempting to deceive others, and this does lead to people making social and business exchanges that they might otherwise not make. Posner seems to be correct in saying that the economic case against deception in business is, in apparently relevant ways, applicable to personal interactions as well. Shall we conclude, then, that utilitarians should be opposed to a right of personal privacy (though not, perhaps, to certain ways of trying to gain information)? This is difficult to answer, for we would have to determine the merits of economic analysis, both on its own terms and from the standpoint of more orthodox utilitarian thought, and if it is wanting we would have to examine other utilitarian arguments with respect to privacy. And more to the point, the argument can't be a definitive test of utilitarianism, for some utilitarians might accept the argument against rights of privacy—as, indeed, some non-utilitarians have done. So the most that can be said is that there is some doubt whether utilitarianism provides a basis for at least some of the rights championed by liberals. But in any event, hardly anyone believes in whatever rights they accept on the basis of such arguments—individualistic concerns are much more to the point in the minds of most people.

3

On Having a Right

The aim of this chapter is to try to illuminate the nature of rights, particularly by paying attention to some aspects of the logic of rights and to how rights function in moral argument. The chapter proceeds by noting difficulties in talking about rights when something like the right to life is asserted and then situations occur in which killing or not saving are justified. What has happened to the right? The chapter examines and rejects some popular ways of dealing with this problem, and then offers a new proposal for dealing with it.

Conflicts of Rights

(1) In most theories of rights, rights can come into conflict. If a theory of rights recognizes both a right concerning knowledge and a right of privacy, then apparent conflicts between one person's right to know and another's right of privacy must be dealt with, and likewise for apparent conflicts, in some theories, between property rights and rights of equality, or between one person's right to liberty and another's right not to be harmed, etc. Even if a conflict is not seen as a conflict of rights, there are apparently situations in which rights can be overridden. For example, I have a right to enter my house, but if a terrorist is holding a hostage inside whom he threatens to kill if anyone enters, then something seems to happen to my right to enter. How rights are thought of in such cases has been considered by many to be a matter of some importance for our understanding of rights.

One way of dealing with rights in such cases is by making use of a notion of prima facie rights, by analogy to the notion of prima facie duties. A person has many prima facie rights—such as the right to free speech, the right to privacy, and property rights—that he may exercise or insist on only if they are not outweighed or overridden by other moral considerations which are, in the circumstances, more important. So if, on a particular occasion, my prima facie right to privacy comes into conflict with a newspaperman's (or the public's) right to know, and the latter is, in the circumstances, more important, then, though I have a prima facie right of privacy, I have no actual, or concrete right to privacy in those circumstances.

The foregoing view has been regarded as unsatisfactory because it treats rights as merely provisional or presumptive. The following, from Herbert Morris, indicates quite clearly what the problem is thought to be:

It is seriously misleading to turn all justifiable infringements into noninfringements by saying that the right is only *prima facie*, as if we have in concluding that we should not accord a man his rights, made out a case that he had none. To use the language of *prima facie* rights misleads, for it suggests that a presumption of the existence of a right has been overcome in these cases where all that can be said is that the presumption in favor of according a man his rights has been overcome. (Morris, 1968, 499)

And similarly Joel Feinberg says that rights "are not something that one has only at specific moments, only to lose, regain, and lose again as circumstances shift. Rights are themselves *property*, things we own, and from which we may not even temporarily be dispossessed. Perhaps in some circumstances rights may be rightfully infringed, but that is quite different from their being taken away and then returned." (Feinberg, 1973, 75) The solution is, as these writers see it, to distinguish between according rights and recognizing rights. On the view that rights are prima facie, as they see it, overridden rights are neither accorded nor recognized, whereas the reality of the situation, they say, is that rights are unconditionally recognized even if not always accorded.

That this is the best way of dealing with conflicts involving rights is thought to be confirmed by the fact that it explains how it can be the case that "a person can maintain a right to X even when he is not morally justified in its exercise. . . ." (Feinberg, 1973, 75) A person can be said to have a right in the sense that his right is to be recognized even if he is not permitted to act on it (in the case of a liberty-right) or is not entitled to some performance on the part of another person (in the case of a claim-right).

This, Feinberg says, is "a less paradoxical alternative to the theory of prima facie rights." (Feinberg, 1973, 75) It seems to me, however, that this way of handling conflicts is hardly less paradoxical. Think of the example described above: a terrorist holds a hostage in my house, threatening to kill the hostage if anyone enters. The Feinberg-Morris view says that I have a right to enter my house which is more than just a prima facie right that has been overridden; what's wrong with that idea, they say, is that it implies that I've lost my right—it has, for the moment, gone out of existence—whereas in fact I still have that right. Very well, then, imagine me walking up to my door. A policeman blocks my way, saying that I may not enter. I say, "It's my house, isn't it," and the policeman says, "Yes, it is." I then say, "So I can enter it," and he says, "No, you can't." Then I say "Since it's my house I have the right to enter, don't I," and he agrees that I do. I continue with "So that means that I have the real, actual, no-fooling right, here and now, at this instant, to enter my house," and he again agrees. So I say, "All right, here I go," but as I start toward the door, I am again blocked and met with the reply "Sorry, you can't go in there."

Needless to say, it seems to me to be extraordinary to maintain that I have a right, then and there, to enter my house. This is not a case of having a right to do something where one nevertheless shouldn't do it. If I have some popcorn, and you would like some, perhaps I should give you some, but I don't have to do so—I have the right not to give you any, and it's up to me whether to give you some or not. But in the hostage case it's not up to me whether or not I enter my house. Even if there is no one to prevent my entering, it's not up to me. I am morally required not to enter. In short, I have no right to enter. It's a contradiction to maintain both that I have a right, then and there, to enter and that I am, then and there, morally required not to enter.

There is at least one common linguistic expression that to my ear suggests this idea—namely, the notion of being "within one's rights" in doing something. If I were to ask whether I would be within my rights in entering my house in the circumstances, the quite proper answer would be that I would not, and this seems to me to be just another way of saying that I do not have the right to enter in the circumstances.

(2) How about the theory of prima facie rights as a way of dealing with conflicts—is it a good theory? Well, it does give an account of conflicts, as follows. Assuming, for the sake of discussion, that there are rights on the opposing sides of free press/fair trial issues, we could say that there is a prima facie right of the public to know certain things, and also a prima facie right of individuals to privacy, and that in some cases these prima facie rights come into conflict. When this happens there must be some mechanism for determining which right in the situation is to prevail. The individual with the dominant prima facie right is then said to have an actual or concrete

right, whereas the individual with the dominated prima facie right has no actual or concrete right. This account of conflicts differs from the one discussed in the previous section only in that it does not maintain that the individual with the dominated right still has a right in the situation, which exists in being recognized even though it is not accorded.

The apparatus of prima facie rights can also be deployed if it is held that rights can be overridden by things other than competing rights. Someone might say that in the case of the hostage in my house, my prima facie right to enter is outweighed not by a competing right, but because in the circumstances not much is lost if I am kept out for a while, whereas very bad consequences will occur if I enter. As a result, my prima facie right is overridden, and in the circumstances I have no actual, or concrete, right to enter.

If the idea of balancing competing prima facie rights is to be plausible, though, certain lines of thought must be avoided. To get into the spirit of this sort of rights-theory, we must keep in mind that we are attempting to find a basis for justifying certain behavior. Someone wants to do something (or have someone else do something), and claims to have an actual, or concrete right to do it (or have it done), and he claims this on the basis of a general prima facie right authorizing his behavior. If others have rights, he claims that his right overrides theirs. Now what is essential in this is that this person is claiming that it is just the possession of the general prima facie right that justifies his behaving as he does (for what is a theory of rights about, if not the justification of behavior, or of demands made on others). But, of course, his prima facie right will adequately support his behavior only if it prevails over any competing prima facie rights had by others. It is very important for a theory of rights to explain how this is accomplished.

Consider a case of peeping through someone's bedroom window to see what he or she looks like undressed. Suppose someone were to say, "Clearly it is not permissible for you to do that, so in this instance the right to privacy prevails over the right to know." Formally, I suppose, this is compatible with a framework of rights: the prima facie right of privacy prevails over the prima facie right to know, and therefore there is an actual, concrete, right in the circumstances not to be looked at. But there is a problem. How has it been determined which right prevails in the situation? If it has been determined that the right of privacy is to prevail on the ground that it is wrong to peep into the window, then the appeal to rights adds nothing, for then we cannot explain in terms of a general prima facie right that someone possesses, *why* it is wrong to peep through that window. For the judgment that it is wrong was made independently, and *then* it was determined that the prima facie right of privacy outweighs the prima facie right to know. (See Thompson, 1976, 12.)

The upshot of this is that if prima facie rights are to do any work, they must not only function as premises in a formal argument whose conclusion says that we have a concrete right to do something, or have something done, but they must also actually be the moral items that are consulted in reaching the conclusion. And this means that we must be able to explain exactly how it is to be determined which prima facie right is to prevail.

One possibility is to establish a hierarchy of prima facie rights in terms of their strengths, such that a prima facie right of one kind would always prevail over one of another kind. But there is little hope for this, for it seems very obviously not the case that, for example, the right of privacy always prevails over, or is always trumped by, the right to know. Indeed, it is doubtful that there is a permanent ordering of any two prima facie rights—it all seems to depend on the circumstances.

A more promising line of thought is to identify the interests underlying prima facie rights, and then to identify the weight of a prima facie right with the importance of the interest. We will ignore the fact that there can be a constellation of interests, and not just one interest, served by a prima facie right. Now there are at least two ways in which the balancing of such prima facie rights might proceed. First, as J. L. Mackie sees it,

the rights we have called fundamental can be no more than *prima facie* rights: the rights that in the end people have, their final rights, must result from compromises between their initially conflicting rights. These compromises will have to be worked out in practice, but will be morally defensible only insofar as they reflect the equality of the *prima facie* rights. This will not allow the vital interests of any to be sacrificed for the advantage of others, to be outweighed by an aggregate of less vital interests. Rather we might think in terms of a model in which each person is represented by a point-center of force, and the forces (representing *prima facie* rights) obey an inverse square law, so that a right decreases in weight with the remoteness of the matter on which it bears from the person whose right it is. There will be some matters so close to each person that, with respect to them, his rights will nearly always outweigh any aggregate of other rights, though admittedly it will sometimes happen that issues arise in which the equally vital interests of two or more people clash. (Mackie, 1978, 356)

But the notion of a vital interest is unclear. If an interest is vital just in case it ought to prevail in the circumstances, then the account of how prima facie rights are balanced is circular, for we are no longer saying that a given prima facie right should prevail because it is the weightiest, but instead that it is weightiest because it should prevail. But if the importance of an interest is determined independently, then it is not the case that the vital interests of one individual cannot be "outweighed by an aggregate of less vital interests" of others. For sometimes marginal impacts on interests such as health or privacy must give way to less weighty interests and even to the convenience of others.

The balancing of prima facie rights in terms of the weight of interests might, instead, go as follows. We might take account of all the interests affected in the situation, and the degree to which they will be affected, and then decide that the actual, or concrete, right (the "final" right, as Mackie calls it) is possessed by one of the parties just in case its existence would maximize the promotion and preservation of interests. One would expect, in balancing prima facie rights in this way, that any given prima facie right would prevail sometimes but could be outweighed on other occasions, which accords with our sense of things.

But there are problems. For one thing, if this is the way rights function, no sense can be given to the idea of having an actual, or concrete, right that ought not to be exercised (in the case of liberties) or insisted upon (in the case of claims). For if there were interests that counted, on balance, against exercising (or insisting on) a right, then on the theory of prima facie rights as here interpreted there would be no actual, or concrete, right in the first place. The conflict would have been resolved in favor of the competing interests, and there would have been no actual, or concrete, right in the first party at all.

Second, it would appear that when prima facie rights are balanced in this way, the actual, or concrete, right will always be the one that maximizes utility. The problem with this is that it seems to many, including myself, that rights can be counter-utilitarian—indeed, I would say that one not only may exercise a right when it would be better if he didn't, but can even *have* a right when it would be better if he didn't. And further, if rights are never counter-utilitarian, one is led to wonder whether there is a need to talk about rights at all. Rights would seem to be redundant if they functioned in this way, for it would be possible to dispense entirely with the notion of rights in carrying on our moral business.

The Conclusory Role of Rights

(3) In this section I want to discuss what seems to me the proper way in which rights enter into moral reasoning. From the preceding sections we can identify some conditions of adequacy for an account

of the role of rights in moral reasoning. The kinds of reasoning about rights that we have so far considered fail to meet these conditions, and I will try to locate the cause of the failures.

The first condition of adequacy is that it must be the case that if a person has a right at a time t, then he is within his rights in acting, or insisting, on his right. And that means that *if* the right exists at t, then it cannot be overridden, or non-accorded, or in any way made inoperative except as the right-holder wishes not to act, or insist, on it. (We do not need to discuss here the mechanisms of waiver.) And this means, I think, that a right that one has at time t is absolute.

Second, the having of a right at a time t must be compatible with the idea that it might be the case that one ought not to exercise, or insist on, his right. Third, rights must make a distinctive contribution to moral reasoning, in the sense that the question of whether a person has a right at a time t cannot (or at least cannot always) be entirely determined by whether, based on the circumstances at t, his having that right at t is for the best. Finally, if actual, concrete, or final rights are derived from general (perhaps prima facie) rights, it must be the case that people can actually figure out what their concrete rights are by thinking about, weighing and balancing where necessary, their general (prima facie) rights.

Neither the theory of prima facie rights, nor the theory of rights as being recognized but not accorded, satisfies the conditions of adequacy. The former theory fails on all counts, and the latter fails to satisfy the last three conditions. The main problem, however, is with the last condition—that is, with the way in which these theories bring rights into moral reasoning.

Let us think of the question of whether a person has the right to do some particular act A on a given occasion (or, in the case of claim-rights, whether N has the right to someone else doing a particular act A). We will call the assertion that N has the right to do a particular act A a particular right-assertion—previously we have spoken of actual, or concrete, or final rights. Such assertions are defended, within the framework we have been looking at, by pointing to one of the general rights that N has: N has the right to do A because doing A is a case of, say, speaking freely, and one of N's rights is the right to speak freely. In this bit of moral reasoning rights come in in two ways—in the conclusion (the conclusory role) and as reasons, or premises (the justificatory role).

Now given the problems that this sort of reasoning has with the conditions of adequacy, it seems to me that it is a mistake to invoke rights in a justificatory role—that is, to think that we have a (general) right to speak freely *in the sense that* it is *because* we have this right that we have the right actually to do a given particular act. Perhaps we should instead regard a right like the (general) right to speak freely as derivative from particular right-assertions. Nonparticular right-assertions might be regarded as merely summaries of kinds of particular acts that we often are actually within our rights in doing or insisting on, and these particular right-assertions would not be regarded as being backed up or justified by nonparticular right-assertions. This is not to say that there are no reasons supporting particular right-assertions. There are certain important and morally relevant considerations that constitute reasons for particular right-assertions, and whose relevance in supporting such right-assertions is independent of their character as rights—which they have only in a summary way, in that they summarize kinds of acts that we often have the actual right to do.

This proposal is not, however, a rejection of rights. Rights do exist—as the conclusions, but not the premises, of certain arguments. What the point of rights is, if they do not serve as ultimate reasons, will be taken up in section 5.

(4) There are other distinctions concerning rights which, at first blush, seem similar to the distinction observed in the last section between general and particular rights. We should be clear as to what these are, so as to avoid confusions.

(a) H. L. A. Hart has made a distinction between general and special rights. (Hart, 1955, 183-188) A special right, according to Hart, is a right arising out of a special transaction or relationship. For example, rights arising under contracts, or the rights of children arising within the family, are special rights. General rights are simply rights not arising out of any special transaction or relationship—an example is the right to liberty.

This distinction is quite different from the general/particular distinction drawn in section 3. For a right that is general in Hart's sense can be particular—if one is at liberty (to use Hart's example of a general right) to do A on some particular occasion, that right need not arise out of any special transaction or relationship. Also, a right that is special in Hart's sense—such as the right of a child against a parent—could be general in the sense explained in section 3, in that it might not be some child's actual, concrete right on a particular occasion.

It is not clear why Hart offered a distinction which appears to concern only the genesis of rights. Perhaps the difference he meant to draw our attention to is that between a right that one has against some determinate individual, and a right that one has against no one, or against everyone, or against indeterminate individuals.

(b) There is a distinction between a right *in rem* and a right *in personam,* and this might be understood as a general/particular distinction. One way of explaining the *in rem/in personam* distinction is to think of it as a distinction between a right to property and a right against an individual. Ownership of a piece of land is *in rem,* whereas a right to payment from some determinate individual under a contract is *in personam.* This is not everyone's conception of an *in rem* right, however. Hohfeld, among others, thought of an *in rem* right (say, to a piece of land) as a large package of *in personam* rights—rights against every individual with respect to the land. (Hohfeld, 1919, 72)

Whatever the proper account of *in rem* rights, it is clear that the *in rem/in personam* distinction is different from the general/particular distinction of section 3. As shown above, a right against some determinate individual can be general in the sense of section 3, if it can be overridden—that is, if it might not be one's actual, concrete right on a particular occasion. And a right against everyone, or a right that exists without being against anyone, can be particular in that one has it and can act on it, or insist on it, on a particular occasion, there being no considerations defeating his claim to do so.

Ought and Obligation

(5) Several references have been made in this book to the idea that a person can have a right that he ought not to exercise (in the case of liberties) or insist on (in the case of claims). It will be worthwhile focusing on this idea, for it seems to me that in it we can discover what is central in a person's claim to have a right with respect to something. First we need to be clear about the sense of ought in which one can have a right that he ought not to exercise.

The word "ought" in ordinary usage is rather imprecise; it seems to be used in three different ways. First, one who says "John ought to help" might be saying that when everything that is relevant in the situation has been taken into account, John is morally required to help. There are two elements of this moral claim that need to be highlighted: the judgment is an "all-in" one, the outcome of having considered everything having a bearing in the matter; and it is a judgment to the effect that something is morally *required.* Second, one who says "John ought to help" might be saying this as a kind of sub-conclusion. Certain considerations might be taken to support the view that he should help, but not be decisive. This might come out as the thought that John ought to help, other things being equal; or that prima facie he ought to help; or that he has a prima facie obligation to help. As in the previous case, it is moral *requirement* that is ultimately at issue, and so the claim that John ought to help would amount to the claim that prima facie John is morally required to help, or that there is a prima facie moral requirement that John help, etc. Third, one who says "John ought to help" might be saying that John should help even though he is not morally required to do so. This might be said in different ways: "If John were a good person, he would help"; "It would be nice of John to help"; "John should help even though he doesn't have to"; and especially "John should not stand on his rights—he should help."

Usage of "ought', "obligation", and related terms is not very precise, even among philosophers, and it is not my purpose to insist that certain uses of these words are correct or even best. Rather, what I want to do is point out that there is an important distinction in morals which can be expressed by appropriate uses of these words. It is the distinction between what is morally required of a person, and what a person should do even though he doesn't have to (morally speaking). I propose to use the word "obligation" to mean a moral requirement, and "ought" in cases where one should, but doesn't have to, do something. It will also be true of this use of "obligation" that to say someone has an obligation to do something means that he does not have a right not to do it—whereas to say merely that he ought to do it is compatible with his having a right not to do it. All of this requires further elucidation.

Suppose that someone asks me for a match to light a cigarette, or for the time, and it would be no trouble at all for me to comply with the request. I ought to do either of these things, it would be good of me to do so, but I have the right not to do so. Or, to borrow an example of Judith Thomson's, if I have some chocolate ice cream, and have eaten all I want, and you would like the rest, I ought to give it to you, but I don't have to—I would be within my rights if I buried it in my garden. (Thomson, 1975, 297) Or someone, perhaps a stranger to me, needs a ride to catch a train, and it would hardly be out of my way; perhaps I ought to help, but it is not required of me.

In the foregoing examples something even stronger can be said. There may be every reason to give the match, or the ice cream, or the ride, and no reason not to do so except that I don't want to. But however one expands the "I don't want to," the point is that it certainly could be the case that in each example the reasons in favor of doing the act in question outweigh the reasons (if there are any) against doing the act—and yet it is still the case that I don't have to do it. Sometimes the reasons for acting might be so powerful that I do have to act, but I am focusing on cases where this is not so.

There is, to be sure, the appearance of paradox in the above, for what is being asserted in the examples is that even though the strongest considerations relevant in each situation support my acting in a certain way, nevertheless I will be justified in not so acting, and the justification for my refusing to help in these cases comes from the same morality that says that the strongest considerations relevant in the situation yield the conclusion that I should help. But though this is paradoxical, it is often the case, and is important in understanding rights. What a morality must provide, it seems to me, is an ought/obligation distinction in which "ought"-judgments are backed by moral considerations that, in a given set of circumstances, favor but do not require an act, and in which "obligation"-judgments are backed by moral considerations that point toward a given act (or omission) being required. Such a distinction is essential to understanding rights because while it is not contradictory to say that N has a right to do (or insist on) A though he ought not to do so, it is contradictory to say that N has a right to do (or insist on) A though he has an obligation not to do so.

Two suggestions as to how to make the distinction can be found in John Stuart Mill's *Utilitarianism*, as recently interpreted by David Lyons. (Lyons, 1976 and 1977) Mill distinguishes between duty and expedience, and though this is not exactly an obligation/ought distinction, it may be analogous and useful. (We will here take "duty" and "obligation" to be interchangeable.) It is not exactly an obligation/ought distinction because Mill regards duty as exhaustive of morality, so that judgments of expedience (judgments about what is "inexpedient, undesirable, or regrettable" [Lyons, 1977, 119]) are not moral judgments. They are nevertheless value judgments, and so may suggest a way for us to distinguish what one is obligated to do from what one ought to do but does not have to do. Mill makes the distinction between duty and expedience in terms of whether the behavior in question should be exacted by means of a sanction (Mill, 1957, 60): if so, it is a duty; if not, expedience. Whether sanctions should be imposed is, for Mill, a matter of the utility of so doing, and he is aware that the imposition of sanctions itself has utilitarian costs. However, and against Mill, if all of the sanctions to be employed are external sanctions, then it seems likely that some things we regard as moral obligations—things one has to refrain from doing—will not turn out to be obligatory, such as a good bit of honesty and truth-telling. Mill meets this, according to Lyons, by including internal sanctions: something is a matter of duty if and only if utility would be promoted by bringing it about that people suffer "reproaches of conscience" on doing or even thinking about doing certain acts. But if this is Mill's view, then it is not clear that he has a duty/expedience distinction, for it is not evident that such sanctions should not, on grounds of utility, be internalized even with respect to so-called matters of expedience. We do, after all, impose informal social sanctions and encourage the internalization of behavior constraints with respect to some matters of etiquette and politeness without regarding these as elements of moral duty.

Another suggestion derived from Mill is that an obligation/ought distinction might, with some modification, be analogous to the distinction between duties of perfect and of imperfect obligation. Mill regards both of these as sanctionable kinds of acts (and hence duties); perhaps, though, we can regard the latter as not being obligations at all, but rather a matter of what one ought but need not do. This would, indeed, give us an obligation/ought distinction. However, it would not be an appropriate one, for in some cases in which a person merely ought not to do something (but has no obligation not to do it) there is a specifiable individual who is "wronged" (affected disadvantageously or not affected advanta-geously), yet this does not turn "ought to do" into "obligated to do".

Yet another possible way of making an obligation/ought distinc-tion is to say that obligations exist only where there has been a prior act or event, such as an agreement or the acceptance of a benefac-tion, or else where there is an office or station imposing some task on the officeholder. (Brandt, 1964, 386) Then "ought"-judgments would be moral judgments that are not of this kind. However, though the foregoing account of obligation may constitute cores of the notion of obligation and duty, at least historically, there appear to be perfectly legitimate extended uses of these notions (e.g., the duty or obligation to help someone in dire need) in which these special elements are missing and all that is left is the general sense that to say that one has an obligation is to say that he has to do the thing in question. (Brandt, 1964, 390 and elsewhere)

(6) An "obligation"-judgment says that one has to do something, that from a moral standpoint one's options are closed. An "ought"-judgment, by contrast, is one that does not foreclose one's moral options. Sanction theories of obligation make the mistake of holding that a directive for behavior can be an obligation-imposing directive (a "have to do" directive) only if it makes provision for something that will motivate compliance, or at least aims at motivating compliance. And it is an error of a similar sort to confuse what an "obligation"-judgment *says* (that one has to do A) with the question of how such judgments are to be established. If we want to know of a particular act A whether N is obligated to do it or merely ought to do it, we need a theory of justification telling us what establishes these

judgments. But it is not the different justifications that distinguish them; it is differences in the kinds of judgments they are. It is because they are different that their justifications differ.

An "obligation"-judgment, to repeat, narrows one's morally allowable options; an "ought"-judgment says that someone has discretion, a prerogative, an option, and leaves it up to the person what he will do. Contrast, for example, "I have an obligation to punish you" and "I ought to punish you, but I don't have to (and I won't)." The point of an "obligation"-judgment is to say that the possible options in a given situation have been reduced by morally relevant considerations to the point that only one is a morally acceptable choice. "Obligation"-judgments thus have an aspect of coercion about them; they are not actually coercive, but neverthe-less they are designed (so to speak) to have an indirect effect on one's will. This is why we often regard what we see as our duty as something that is not of our own choice and not within our control. We see ourselves as coerced by what we regard as our obligations, or even as "determined" by them. Existentialists call this bad faith, but whatever we make of that criticism and the metaethics on which it rests, it does not show that that is not what the concept of obligation is all about.

So the situation is this. Sometimes there are moral considerations that leave us no options as to what we are to do, while in other cases, though there may be moral considerations favoring one act rather than another, we have an option as to what to do—both when others have obligations with respect to us and it is up to us whether we will insist on performance, and when we have a right (liberty) to do something and it is up to us whether to exercise our right. The question is *why* our morality leaves room for such options, given that there are moral considerations favoring one outcome rather than another. Obviously, where one has a right to do what he ought not to do, one is morally justified in resisting certain moral consider-ations. Why does, or should, a morality do this? Why not require people always to act in accordance with the weight of the relevant moral considerations? Why not require people always to come up to the most exacting moral standards?

Perhaps the way this last question has been formulated suggests possible answers. It might be too great a burden to impose on people to expect each and every bit of behavior to measure up to the highest standards. It might not even be possible, given certain aspects of human personality, for people on the whole to come up to such standards, even though some might be able to do so all of the time and all some of the time; and yet it hardly seems appropriate in all such cases to resort to the mechanism of excuses in a context of obligations. Another possible reason is that allowing such options provides an avenue for self-assertion within a framework of requirements often seen and felt as oppressive and quasi-coercive; this is a sort of safety-valve argument. Related to this, though, is the consideration that a too-demanding morality would frustrate individual goals and life plans. To pursue one's own life plan one must not always (i.e., regularly and continually) be imposed upon by the demands of others; one must be able to foresee the sorts of occasions on which he will be called upon to think about things other than his own projects so that he can plan accordingly, and these demands must not be so frequent that they virtually destroy the possibility of planning for them. It is for reasons such as this that simple utilitarianism is seen as too demanding a morality. It makes everything a moral matter in the sense that it obligates in every instance. There is another relevant way in which simple utilitarianism contrasts with a morality that recognizes rights. To recognize rights is to recognize a way of accomodating the individual self within morality. Simple utilitarianism builds in the self, but in one way, as seen above, it does not give it enough weight (or room), while in another respect ("everyone counts") it gives it too much weight, for it might allow one to break promises if slightly greater good could thereby be produced, even if the beneficiary of that increment is the agent himself. (The notion of a duty to oneself, on the other hand, does get the self into morality, but not only is the notion of such an obligation doubtful, it seems not to allow one to prefer himself to the extent that we do seem entitled to prefer ourselves.) There is one further reason for a morality not insisting on observance of the most exacting standards. Recognizing oughts that are not obligations allows praise to operate as a regular form of moral motivation. Though obligations are not logically connected with sanctions, still, some sort of adverse response is appropriate and likely for failures to fulfill obligations, and is likely to be a significant factor in moral motivation. One can, indeed, praise people for fulfilling their obligations, and such praise can serve to motivate, but where there are oughts that are not obligations praise will be a normal and regular form of motivation.

A morality that requires people always to act in accordance with the weight of the relevant moral considerations is a morality in which everything is a matter of obligation and in which there are no oughts. Such a morality has little use for rights. It will, to be sure, have permissions: if one has no obligation to do A, he is permitted not to do A, and if one has no obligation not to do A, then he is permitted to do A. But in a morality of obligation people will seldom have bilateral permissions (that is, permission to do A and permission not to do A), for these will exist only when the moral considerations supporting an obligation to do A and those support- ing an obligation not to do A are evenly balanced, and this is not likely to be very often—certainly not as often as we would suppose people to be morally permitted to do or refrain from doing some- thing. So for the most part, in a morality without oughts there would be no place for rights, since for (almost) every act it would either be obligatory to do it or obligatory not to do it. Rights thus have a genuine place in morality only if not (virtually) everything is a matter of obligation; only if, that is, some things are a matter of individual prerogative; in a word, only if there are oughts. To have a right is to have a sufficient justification for exercising a prerogative, i.e., for deciding whether to do A (or to insist on A's being done by another) even if the best reasons, though not demonstrating an obligation not to do A, favor not doing it.

(7) The central distinction in the moral outlook presented here is between the part of a person's life which is, morally speaking, within his control (in the sense that morality permits him to choose what to do), and the part which isn't. The latter is the realm of obligation; the former is the realm of, at most, oughts but not of obligations.

Something can be obligatory for a person in one of two sorts of ways, which I will call the direct and the indirect. I do not have a theory of directly created obligations to offer, but examples include promises and other voluntary undertakings, unjust enrichments, and others. Obligations are created indirectly when other sorts of morally relevant considerations (including considerations of wel- fare and well-being, and certain aspects of justice) mount up and grow to such a pitch that they result in an individual *having* to behave in a given way. Again, I do not have a theory of such considerations, and am arguing by example.

At this point some comments will be helpful. The first comments have to do with considerations that can yield obligations indirectly. For one thing, I am assuming that these considerations are in some way additive—that however incommensurable they may seem in principle, it is somehow possible to do something along the following lines: add some increment of welfare, subtract some loss of justice, and decide whether on the whole there is an improve- ment. Second, as the example indicates, the considerations need not be only of the utilitarian sort, involving only welfare and well-being; this will be pursued in chapter 6. Third, I take it that there is nothing particularly troublesome about saying that the considerations we are talking about may be such that, singly or in combination, they do not add up to a case strong enough to impose a moral requirement on someone, but, on the other hand, may sometimes be strong enough, singly or in combination, that a moral requirement results.

There is just one comment concerning directly created obligations—namely that the occurrences which sometimes give rise to these obligations can be outweighed or overridden, so that the obligation does not arise. The difference between this and indirectly created obligations is that here the obligation will arise *unless* there are adequate countervailing considerations—i.e., promises, unjust enrichment, and certain other occurrences are always (in themselves and absent other considerations) sufficient to create obligations—whereas with respect to indirectly created obligations the considerations that may add up to an obligation are not the sort which by their nature would always be strong enough (absent countervailing considerations) to create an obligation.

Rights enter this picture in the following way. With respect to liberty rights, there is always a presumption that one may do something if he wishes—this is part of the prerogative, the moral space, discussed earlier. Having such a right does not mean, though, that there are no considerations counting against his doing it. When we say, then, that a person has a right to do something that he ought not to do, what this means is that there is no directly created obligation not to do it, and other relevant considerations, though they count on the whole against doing it, do not add up to an obligation not to do it. With respect to claim-rights, on the other hand, the idea is that the direct or indirect considerations that impose an obligation on someone also justify someone else in insisting on the performance of the obligation, even if the latter shouldn't. The usual case will be one in which the obligation is a directly created one (as, due to a promise), where there are considerations not sufficiently strong to defeat the obligation but which nevertheless count against insisting on it, thus bringing it within the area of one's prerogative. An interesting, and problematic, case of an indirectly created obligation is the so-called duty to rescue—which will be discussed in chapters 5 and 8.

When a case of the foregoing sort arises, we are faced with a situation in which a claim about what a person is entitled to do or have done conflicts with a claim about what he ought to (but doesn't have to) do—conflicts, that is, in the sense that the claims point to different behavior. In such a case it is entirely up to the agent what he or she does. It is not, however, up to the agent merely in the sense that everyone must make his or her own assessment of what is right and wrong; rather, it is up to the agent in the sense that if the agent chooses in accordance with his right, and not with what he ought to do, his choice will have an adequate moral justification. He will be *morally* justified in resisting certain *moral* considerations—

and it is, indeed, a matter of resisting, and not a case of the latter considerations being overridden.

There are two additional remarks to be made at this point. To have a right is to be in a position in which one is justified in behaving in a given way even if one ought not to do so, or to be justified in insisting on someone else acting in a given way even if one ought not to insist. But it is important to be clear, with respect to the latter, that it is not the case that I am justified in insisting *because* the other person has an obligation, or that the other person has an obligation *because* I am justified in insisting. Instead, in the usual case there is a set of considerations supporting *both* my having a right and also some other person's having an obligation. But there can be cases in which the relevant considerations support the other person's obligation but in which I am not justified in insisting on its performance. Suppose, for example, that though you owe Jones money, you are unaware of this, and Jones waits an exceedingly long time to make you aware of your debt. It seems to me that we could come to the conclusion that you do owe Jones the money, but at the same time that Jones has waited so unconscionably long in presenting his claim that he is not justified in insisting on payment. There can also be cases in which the relevant considerations justify me in insisting on something, but do not, at least at the moment, obligate anyone, or anyone in particular—as, for example, where I have contractual rights but the contracting party has died.

The final point to be made here is this. Bentham once decried the idea of rights (more precisely, "The natural and imprescriptible rights of man") on the ground that they are anarchical, in that government and orderly society would be impossible if these so-called rights were to be honored. (Bentham, 1843: in Melden, 28-39) Critics have rightly pointed out that Bentham overstated the case, for he thought that these rights must be "unbounded" and absolute. But whatever the merits of Bentham's actual charges, there is a sense in which rights are indeed anarchical—namely that they permit, and their existence even encourages, selfishness when sacrifice may be needed. There are many occasions on which the world, or some small part of it, would be better if people would forgo their rights, and yet morally speaking they do not have to.

4

Rights and the Duty to Compensate

In the preceding chapter it was maintained that one can't say that he has a right, then and there, to do something if he is not permitted, then and there, to do it. Another way of putting this is to say that a right doesn't exist if one can't act on it (or insist on it). Recently an important argument has been developed by a number of writers challenging this and in support of what is called the infringement theory of rights. The aim of this chapter is to develop and then to answer the main argument for that theory.

The idea of the infringement theory is this: A person, we would say, has a right of some sort—for example, a right not to be killed, or a right not to have a piece of property appropriated. Sometimes, however, it is permissible to act contrary to such rights—we may kill an innocent aggressor or eat someone's food without permission if these are necessary to preserve our lives. The following passage from Joel Feinberg presents a useful case for discussion:

Suppose that you are on a back-packing trip in the high mountain country when an unanticipated blizzard strikes the area with such ferocity that your life is imperiled. Fortunately, you stumble onto an unoccupied cabin, locked and boarded up for the winter, clearly somebody else's private property. You smash in a window, enter, and huddle in a corner for three days until the storm abates. During this period you help yourself to your unknown benefactor's food supply and burn his wooden furniture in the fireplace to keep warm. Surely you are justified in doing all these things, and yet you have infringed the clear rights of another person. (Feinberg, 1978, 102)

The important question raised by this example is: What has happened to the cabin owner's right? One move might be to deny that my burning of his furniture is contrary to his right. We might say that he had no right not to have his furniture burned in these

51

circumstances—that is, that his only right was (and is) not-to-have-his-furniture-burned-unjustly, and since my burning it was not unjust, I have not acted contrary to his right.*

There is yet another, less awkward, move. Essentially it amounts to denying that there are rights at all in these cases. We might say, as a first shot, that the moral principles applicable in such situations have entirely to do with the permissible and the impermissible, having no reference whatever to any notion of rights. But we need not go quite this far—perhaps we can say instead that there are rights after all, but that they are determined by what the permissibilities are (and not *vice verse*). So, though you don't have the right not to have your furniture burned when I am permitted to burn it, nevertheless you do generally have that right. But this move won't help a theory of rights, for then the rights have no moral force; it is not they that determine that, or explain why, certain things are permissible and others not.

One of the nice things about the foregoing suggestions is that they result in a certain simplification in morals (or at least it is so claimed), for if the permissibilities control, then we avoid so many apparently intractable clashes of rights. And examples like Feinberg's would not force us to say things like "Yes, you do have a right that your furniture not be burned, but it's outweighed on this occasion, and furthermore, though you have the right (privilege) of preventing others from destroying your property, you may not prevent my doing so on this occasion."

But however nice it would be to avoid these difficulties, infringement theorists reject, in Thomson's words, "the view that rights do not have an independent bearing in the moral assessment of action." (Thomson, 1980, 7) For that is what some of the ways of dealing with the problem of what happened to the cabin owner's right amount to. If we determine what his right is by first, and independently, determining what I may or may not do with his food and furniture, then rights do no work, have no force, no "independent bearing in the moral assessment of action." That they have such a bearing is, of course, contrary to the view of rights outlined in the preceding chapter, so we want to see what the infringement theorists have to say on its behalf.

The infringement theorists's view is that rights don't disappear when outweighed; they persist. Even when it is permissible for me to burn your furniture, you have, then and there, the right that I

*Judith Thomson discusses the problems with these moves in Thomson, 1976, 6-12.

(along with everyone else) not burn it. The right has been out-weighed, overridden; it has not prevented, morally speaking, my burning the furniture nor even entitled you to protect it against my burning it; but it exists, then and there, nevertheless. It has not been extinguished; it has been infringed. An act infringes a right if and only if it is a non-wrong act that is contrary to a right. It does not matter if this use of the word "infringe" is partly stipulative; the matter of importance is the idea that a person can still have a right when there are justifiable acts contrary to it.

Infringement theorists have an argument for their position. It's a simple enough argument to state, though most of this chapter will be taken up discussing it. Here are passages from Thomson and from Feinberg:

Surely you *do* have a right that people will not break into your freezer and take a steak. If you had no such right, why would I have to compensate you later for having [permissibly] done so. And surely I do have to compensate you: I have to pay for the damage I caused to the freezer, and I have to replace, or pay you for, the steak I took. (Thomson, 1976, 10-11)

. . . almost everyone would agree that you owe *compensation* to the homeowner for . . . the destruction of his furniture. One owes compensation here for the same reason one must repay a debt or return what one has borrowed. If the other had no right that was infringed in the first place, one could hardly have a duty to compensate him. Perhaps he would be an appropriate object of your sympathy or patronage or charity, but those are quite different from compensation. (Feinberg, 1978, 102)

So the argument is simply that in each example there is a duty to compensate, and that means that there must be a right that has been infringed. The right must exist, despite the justifiability of some-one's acting contrary to it, for otherwise there would be no such duty. Let us remember that we are talking about compensation for the legitimate infringement, not the illegitimate violation, of rights. Violations, too, call for compensation, but then there is no problem about whether the right exists—it certainly does. The argument holds that a right still exists and is the basis for compensation even when one is permitted to infringe it.

The remainder of this chapter is divided into eight sections. Sections 1 through 5 seek to refute the argument just presented. In sections 6 through 8 I argue for a more appropriate basis for duties to compensate.

(1) First of all, compensation can be due even where no right is infringed. Thomson gives as an example a person's duty to compen-sate for the stew he has eaten in a restaurant. The diner has

infringed no right of the restauranteur; rather, mutual implicit promises have been made, and the duty to compensate rests on these.

(2) Second, not all infringements of rights require compensation. Let's suppose there is a right of privacy that can be violated by intruding upon someone's meditations for the purpose of getting his attention. And let's suppose I have fallen and can't get up, and you're the only one around. I take it that it will be permissible for me to infringe your right of privacy so as to get you to help me. But I also take it that no one would suggest that I owe you any compensation because of the infringement of your right.

Someone might, however, say that the reason no compensation is owed is that there is nothing to compensate—it's not like the burning of your chair, where there is an obvious loss to be made good. And further, someone could say that if you still want to meditate, and there is something I can (reasonably) do to re-create the conditions in which you can meditate (by giving you back, as it were, some of your lost meditation, or at least the opportunity for it), then I owe you that as compensation for the infringement of your right.

But there will be cases in which I can't give you back the opportunity for meditation. If then I have no duty to compensate, is this because there is nothing to compensate? But why? There is an interesting situation in the law which offers a good parallel. One who physically injures another must compensate him not only for his "tangible" losses (loss of income, medical bills, etc.), but also for pain and suffering. Of course, the compensation is in cash, inasmuch as the pain cannot be taken away, but it's compensation nevertheless. This shows that in our right-of-privacy example, we can't explain why no compensation is owed merely by saying that there is nothing to compensate, or no way to compensate. (I take it that it makes no difference to the point at issue that there is a violation of a right in the physical injury case, and not merely an infringement.)

Why is it that pain is something that must be compensated, even though a form of compensation must be fabricated? Well, if it is just the fact that a right not to be caused pain has been infringed (in this case, violated), then why shouldn't the infringement of your right of privacy also give rise to a duty on my part to compensate, even though I can't give you back an opportunity to meditate and a form of compensation must be fabricated?

So compensation is possible for the infringement of your right of privacy, and by analogy to the situation in which the law permits the recovery of compensation for pain, we could hold that compensation is due for my invasion of your right of privacy. But it would seem, to the contrary, that there is no duty to compensate in the latter case. I conclude, therefore, that not all infringements of rights require compensation.

(3) Even if compensation can be due when no right is infringed, and even if not all infringements of rights require compensation, nevertheless it is true that in some cases compensation is required when there has been the infringement of a right. Perhaps in *those* cases we can infer the existence of a right that has been infringed from the duty to compensate. Now, given that compensation can be due even when no right is infringed, we cannot strictly infer a right-infringement from the fact that compensation is owed, but perhaps there are cases in which we can, more modestly, argue that we must point to a right-infringement in order to *explain* the owing of compensation.

This line of thought will work, however, only if pointing to a right-infringement would in fact explain the owing of compensation. How might this explanation go? One possibility is that there is a logical or conceptual connection, such that it is part of the notion of a right, or of having a right, that infringements call for compensation. On such a view, if you don't have at least a prima facie right to compensation when someone behaves in certain ways with respect to x, then you haven't really got a right to, or with respect to, x. This will not do, however. It can't be the needed explanation, for inasmuch as it is supposed to be a logical or conceptual connection, if it holds at all, it holds with respect to all rights, and as we have seen in the case of the right of privacy, there can be rights-infringements without there being even a prima facie right to compensation.

(4) Another possibility is that the infringement of a right explains a duty to compensate only for certain kinds of rights, such as property rights. It does seem, after all, that I owe you compensation when I burn your chair, for I have destroyed your property. Now if the notion of property, or of a property right, is to show how infringement of your right explains the fact that compensation is owed, the story must go something like this. When we are talking about property we are not (or not just) talking about a thing (an artifact, an idea, a piece of land, or whatever); we are talking about a set of rights (including claims, privileges, powers, and immunities) that define one's normative relations to others with respect to something. There are many possible combinations of claims, privileges, powers, and immunities that are sufficient to constitute ownership—one might, for example, have the right to sell, consume,

waste, or destroy something, but not the right to use it personally, or one might have the right to manage something and to the income from it, but lack the right to bequeath it. Professor Lawrence Becker calculates that using the eleven "elements" that might be part of ownership there are about 1500 possible combinations that would actually constitute ownership. (Becker, 1977, 21)

Now the infringement of a property right might explain a duty to compensate if it were the case that one of the elements that must be in the bundle of rights constituting property is the right to be compensated for deprivations of the item in question. Absent this right, the idea would be, there is no property at all. The explanation would then run as follows: The chair is your property, so you have a right not to have it burned; but also, since it is your property, you have the right to be compensated when the destruction of the chair infringes one of the *other* rights in the bundle that constitutes the chair as your property; I have infringed your property right by burning the chair; therefore, you have a right to my compensating you; therefore, I have a duty to compensate you.

Of course, on this view my duty to compensate no longer derives "directly" from my infringement of your right not to have the chair burned. It derives from the fact that in infringing this right I infringe your property right, and this includes and thus entails a right to compensation. Nevertheless, this view is inadequate.

First, even if this were to show, for property rights anyway, how the violating of a right could explain a duty to compensate, it is doubtful that there can never be ownership without a right to compensation. If a person had the right to sell, bequeath, destroy, use, give away, derive the income from, and manage an artifact or piece of land, but also had a duty to donate it in certain circumstances, he would be the owner. Encumbered ownership is still ownership; feudal landlords were owners even though there were often certain uses of their land that were limited by their duties to their villeins and to the Church. Similarly, if a person had all of the above-mentioned rights with respect to something, but no right to compensation for permitted destruction, there would be no more reason for denying that he is the owner.

Second, absent a conceptual connection of some sort between property and a right to compensation, it becomes clear that an infringement of a right not to have one's property burned is not in itself adequate to explain a duty to compensate. It looks as though we will have to find some general moral principle to explain that duty. It will say that in such-and-such circumstances, one must compensate. There could, perhaps, be a principle saying simply that whenever one destroys another's property, he must compensate. I don't think there is such a principle, but even if there were, it is important to notice that it would be the existence of this principle, and not the existence of a right not to have one's property destroyed, that would explain the duty to compensate. Of course, property (even understood as a set of rights) does enter the explanation of there being a duty to compensate in particular circumstances, but only to do two things: (1) to show that it's a case where the principle comes into play (i.e., that it's not a case where no compensation is due because there is no ownership), and (2) to show who is entitled to the compensation. The existence of neither a right not to have one's property destroyed, nor other property rights, provides the ground of the duty to compensate; they do not explain why, when there is property involved, compensation is owed. Some remarks on the principles that do govern compensation will be ventured later in this chapter, and in chapter 8.

(5) Rights are important in that their existence makes a moral difference. The difference is not merely that they are thought to back up claims to compensation. They are also supposed to have a role in determining whether we may do the things for which compensation is owed. For example, the fact that you have a right not to have your chair burned is supposed not only to impose on me a duty to compensate you if I burn your chair, but also to count against my burning it in the first place (and indeed sometimes to be a decisive consideration). This is what Thomson expresses as the idea that rights have "an independent bearing in the moral assessment of action." It seems to me though, that the infringement theorists' argument to show the existence of a right having such a bearing does not succeed.

According to infringement theorists, the argument from the duty to compensate proves the existence of a right having both of these aspects. For the argument to succeed, then the following (A) must be true: In certain cases, the fact that I will owe you compensation if I do a certain thing entails that there is a consideration that counts (sometimes decisively) against the permissibility of my doing that thing. The phrase "in certain cases" is intended merely to make A apply only to the cases in which the infringement theorists' argument is supposed to work, for there are other cases, such as the duty to compensate for food eaten in a restaurant, where the owing of compensation does not entail the existence of a reason not to do the act (eat the food) that results in the duty to compensate.

Even limited to the favored cases, however, A is problematic. It is certainly not argued for, and it seems false. Consider cases of stewardship. You own the only well in town, but your ownership is something like that of a public utility in that you may not refuse to allow anyone to draw water. Since it's yours, those who draw water must compensate you. But this does not mean there is a reason that counts against their drawing it. Not only are they permitted to draw it, but you have no right to their not doing so. This is not a case, like ordering food in a restaurant, of an implicit promise to pay if served; since you can't refuse to allow them to have water, you can't, either explicitly or implicitly, enter into a bilateral agreement with respect to the water.

Or consider involuntary exchange, by which I mean an exchange that one person does not wish to make even though he will be compensated, but is nevertheless forced to make. If, for example, I were to take your pen and give you money (say, its market value) for it, even though you didn't want to sell it, that would be an involuntary exchange. A fairly recent legal case presents a situation it will be useful to consider. In *Boomer v. Atlantic Cement Company* (26 N.Y. 2d 219, 257 N.E. 2d 870 (1970)) defendents operated a cement plant from which emanated dirt, smoke, and vibrations that damaged a number of parcels of land. Plaintiffs sued for damages for the injury already caused to their property, and also to enjoin defendants from causing further injury. Defendants argued that if they were forced to desist from producing the dirt, smoke, and vibration, the plant would have to be closed, resulting in the loss of a large investment and of a great many jobs in the area. The court held that plaintiffs were entitled to compensation for the past damage to the land and for all future damage, but not to an injunction. Thus, defendant could continue to injure plaintiffs' property, but would have to pay compensation. This is a forced exchange: defendant is exchanging something (money) with plaintiffs, against plaintiffs' will, for the opportunity to do something to plaintiffs' land.

Infringement theorists would say that the landowners still have the right not to have their land damaged in this way, though the right has been infringed and compensation is due. This is not the language of lawyers, however. Lawyers distinguish betwen property rights and compensation rights. Property rights are enforceable by injunction, and (usually) the only way one can lose a property right (other than by eminent domain—forced exchange with the government) is by selling it. If no injunction will be granted, there is no right. Thus in *Boomer* the court is taken to have said that the landowners do not have (or if they did, they no longer have) a right not to have their property damaged in certain ways. All they have are compensation rights, supportable by damage suits, which amounts to saying that the cement plant is entitled to force exchanges on the landowners. But if all the landowners have are compensation rights, this means that the fact that the cement company will owe compensation for damage does not mean that the fact that it will be causing damage constitutes a reason for not doing it.

Forced exchanges are a moral possibility, in the sense that it is a moral matter whether they are permissible. Some people believe that forced exchanges in the commercial world are appropriate where they are economically efficient, and that they are efficient where there are high transaction costs. For example, if a company wants to open a mill that will pollute, it could purchase from nearby residents the right to pollute. But the costs of negotiating all these contracts would be immense, and there is also the problem of holdouts. So, some say, it's all right for the mill to go ahead and pollute (i.e., it has the right to do so), and then pay damages. Now I'm not endorsing this, but I am saying it's a moral possibility, to be accepted or rejected on its moral merits. The infringement theorists, by contrast, would have us reject it on the basis of a logical argument—that the compensation requirement entails that there is a right that functions as a consideration, perhaps a sufficient one, against doing what will call for compensation.

So far, then, the argument is this: stewardship and forced exchanges are moral possibilities. But the infringement theorists' argument rules them out. So there are reasons counting against the view that there are rights functioning in moral argument in the way in which infringement theorists take them to function (the "independent bearing" thesis). And as we shall see further on, the existence of rights of this kind are not necessary to explain duties to compensate.

(6) Suppose we were to represent the moral situation we have been exercised about as follows: We could say that there is a moral principle that prohibits destroying another's property without adequate reason, and that there are other principles that indicate in general ways the sorts of things that count as adequate reasons. The principles might also say that it matters how valuable the property is to its owner, and other things as well. There is no need to limit the number of applicable principles. Then there would be principles concerning compensation: they would say that in certain sorts of situations one must compensate others, and of course the duty to compensate for burning the chair would be covered by these principles.

These principles need not be ultimate. Probably we could give reasons for them, and in so doing would be appealing to still more general principles. This process would stop somewhere, and it is an open question whether it stops with one principle, or more than one. (See chapter 6.)

Now moral judgment doesn't become any easier when the moral situation is represented in terms of such principles. What is significant, for our present purposes, is that when the moral situation is described in terms of principles like these, the problems that the infringement theorists insist upon don't crop up. There is no need to urge your right not to have your chair burned in order to explain my duty to compensate you, and then go on to maintain that this right exists (only because, on the infringement view of things, it must exist) even when it is permissible for others to act contrary to it and even when the right-holder is not permitted to protect it. These are great logical difficulties. Apparent contradictions are averred, and only because it is said that we can't explain a duty to compensate unless we can find a right that has been infringed.

But all we have to do to avoid the logical problems is abjure the language of rights, at least as it is used by infringement theorists. We need only say that, morally speaking, there are principles allowing the destruction of others' property in certain situations, and there are also principles that require compensation in (at least some of) those situations. There's no logical problem here, and there is no substantive problem either if there are indeed moral principles requiring compensation.

(7) Of course, there are such principles. Let's begin with a variant of an example of Thomson's (Thomson, 1977, 47) used to support the infringement theory. Suppose I badly need some medicine, the only available supply of which is locked in your house. You cannot be reached to get your permission, so I am justified in breaking into your house to get some of it. I must compensate you, though, ostensibly because I have infringed a right of yours.

Suppose, however (and closer to Thomson's actual example), that I need the medicine but am unconscious, and someone else breaks into your house to get the medicine to administer to me. Well, if you have a right that it not be taken, and that right has been infringed, who is it that owes compensation? Who is it that has infringed your right? Thomson says, vaguely, "if *we* go ahead . . . *we* shall have to" (Thomson, 1977, 50) compensate you. Ultimately, of course, it is I who owe compensation, but this begins to strain once again the idea that it is owed because of the infringement of a right, for I personally have not infringed your right. We might appeal to some notion of principal and agent, or some notion of constructive infringement, to deal with this. But once we do this, or, indeed, even feel a need to do it, the infringement theory starts to weaken, for the fact that your right has been infringed is not adequate to explain who owes compensation, and other moral principles must be sought.

But consider yet another variation. I am badly in need of medicine that only you have available. I am unconscious, and cannot request it or promise to repay. You use the medicine on me. (It does not matter, it seems to me, whether or not you think you are morally required to do this, but I will suppose that you are so required and that you do it for this reason.) I think it is morally incumbent on me, when I recover, at least to offer to replace the medicine or to pay you for it. Yet this duty to compensate is not for the infringement of a right of yours. And again, to dredge up an implied promise is only to demonstrate that in reality there are considerations other than either rights-infringements or promising that call for compensation.

The following question now arises: If, somehow or other, getting some of your medicine requires me to compensate you when I have not appropriated it, then might not the appeal to a rights infringement be unnecessary in explaining my duty to compensate when I *have* expropriated it? In each case I wind up with something of yours that you do not give as a gift. It's yours and I have it. It didn't become mine merely by my needing it,* and there is nothing in the character of your ownership that suggests that you hold it in trust for the needy. I have had a benefit, and I have had it at your expense—you have been "de-benefited." It seems to me that in this we have the explanation of my duty to compensate. If I need medicine, and some medicine of mine were available, I would have to use that, and would not be permitted to break into your house to use yours. Having used mine, I would be without a supply of medicine, and you would still have yours. If I had had my own, but had impermissibly used yours anyway, I would have had to make it good—justice would require that I give you mine, so as to bring about the outcome that should have resulted and would have existed had I used my own in the first place. Likewise when I have none and use yours—justice requires that I use part of my assets to acquire some so that I can restore the situation that would have existed had things gone as they should have. This is hardly a complete principle of compensation (about which more shortly), but it is sufficient to show that it does not seem to be the infringement of a right that stands behind compensation in the mooted cases.

Thomson does, to be sure, suggest that there might be a principle

*This hasn't been argued, but I'm supposing it's so since we are taking it that compensation is due and are merely trying to explain that fact.

of unjust enrichment that explains why I must compensate you if I burn your chair. But she considers the injustice to be merely the infringement of your right, and thus has no explanation at all (as she acknowledges). There is, though, another way to understand the injustice here—it's the having, using, destroying, depriving, or whatever of another's property, so long as nothing in the affair made it yours or made it cease to be his. Of course, the question of when it does cease to be his is not settled by this principle of compensation—other principles determine that.

(8) Compensation can be owed either when I am permitted to help myself to something of yours, or when you are required to do or provide something for me. (We are ignoring unpermitted takings.) The principles governing compensation in these cases are the same, having to do simply with the idea that there is a transfer of resources such that one person has an advantage at another's disadvantage (or a benefit at another's loss).

This is not sufficient, however, for there are many cases where it is all right to do something that shifts the balance of advantages without incurring an obligation to compensate. Competitive situations are like this—one person gains, as a result of which another loses, and no compensation is owed. If Jones's sales record leads to his company's promoting him and firing Smith, Jones does not owe Smith anything. If opening a laundromat reduces the value of the smart shops around it, no compensation is owed. (See Keeton, 1959, 414 n. 28.)

A large element of social practice is involved in the question of when compensation is owed. There are different conceptions, often specific to different societies, or to a given society in different economic conditions, regarding what one's material position in life should be determined by—that is, regarding the legitimate ways of acquiring holdings. Societies differ in the extent to which they regard luck and competitive success as reasonable determinants of one's position in life, though I would imagine that all societies permit both of these to operate to some extent.

Principles of compensation are not principles that determine the legitimate bases for people's material positions. Rather, they accept as given those ideas, and concern certain alterations in material positions that are *not* among the ones by which a person's material position in a society is legitimately determined. In a competitive society such as ours, advancement or business success that adversely affect others, and might even be cases of getting an advantage at another's disadvantage, are legitimate ways of gaining a material position. Hence, principles of compensation do not apply.

But gains at another's expense that are not legitimated by principles of the foregoing sort are unjust enrichments, for which restitution must be made. The idea is this: Acting in accordance with principles legitimating material holdings, people come to have a set of holdings. Think of a set of holdings at a given time as a norm. Deviations from the norm that are not legitimated by the principles just referred to, even though the act causing the deviation is legitimated by other principles, must be erased by a transfer from the one enriched to the one at whose expense the enrichment has been gained. (It is, however, possible that other methods of re-creating the norm could be used, such as taxation and redistribution.)

The notion of gaining at another's expense includes not only the obvious case where I use some of your resources (your chair, your medicine), whether I take them or you respond to an obligation to provide them, but also to the case in which you provide me services. Suppose I am unconscious and you, a doctor who happens to be on the scene, provide me essential medical services. I have gained, but have you lost? I think you have, or if you haven't, then someone else has, for suppose I had been able to get to your (or some other doctor's) office. Professional services would have been provided and paid for, and you or some other doctor would have been richer and I would have been poorer. This is the outcome that should have existed and would have existed had I been able to get to a doctor's office, and I am now richer than I should be because I could not. So a transfer is now called for to produce the appropriate outcome.

There are two additional points to bring up in connection with compensation. First, there can be an obligation to provide some good or service *gratis.* Such obligations often exist among members of a family. And in general non-professionals are not entitled to compensation for the time and effort they expend in fulfilling obligations to help others, though if something—say, a business deal—were lost, the case for compensation would be stronger.

Second, there is a problem with officiousness. People can't volunteer services or goods that would not be welcome and then claim to be entitled to compensation. So a way must be found to distinguish such behavior from that which is entitled to compensation. One possibility is to say that there is an entitlement if the recipient would have agreed to having the goods and services provided. There is a difficulty with this, however—sometimes one agrees to accept goods or services only because of who it is that is offering them (perhaps a friend, or a child one wants to encourage). We can say, then, that there is an entitlement to compensation only if the recipient would have agreed even if almost anyone else had offered the goods or services. In the end, then, it is the character of the benefit—its essentiality for the recipient—that determines whether compensation is due.

5

The Right to Beneficence

Are there rights to beneficence, to welfare? Absent some special relationship, do I ever have a right to others coming forward on my behalf, either by doing something for me, or providing me something I need? No doubt it would be a good thing if others were to help me, but have I a right to it? One division among rights is between so-called positive rights, rights *to* something, as distinct from rights *not* to have something done, which are called negative rights. The latter rights are easier to honor, for one needs only to avoid behaving in certain ways. But the former require coming forward for the benefit of others. Such rights are not thought to be worrisome when they rest on promises and contractual agreements and on other special relationships, but they are hotly contested when it comes to disinterested beneficence.

There appear to be two contexts in which positive rights are seriously in question. On the one hand, some people hold that there are so-called social, or economic, rights. These include some of the rights mentioned in such manifestoes as the United Nations Universal Declaration of Human Rights: the right to work, the right to food, to housing, to medical care, and to education. Rights such as these are distinguished from political and civil rights such as those referred to in the United States Declaration of Independence and Constitution. They are rights of recipience—that is, rights to things not yet possessed. The significant aspect of these rights, for present purposes, is that they are rights that governments, not private individuals, are called upon to satisfy.

There are, on the other hand, situations in which the question arises as to whether a person has a right to a private individual's doing something for him or providing him some resource. For example, if I am drowning, and you can help, do I have a right to your help? Or, if I am starving, do I have a right to your providing me food that you can spare? Or would both of these be merely supererogatory acts, that is, non-required acts of a Good Samaritan who may, if he wishes, withhold them?

The main question in this chapter is whether there are rights that call upon private individuals to act for someone's benefit. As we shall see, the theory of general rights (rights in a justificatory role) has had a great deal to do with some of the views that have been expressed on the matter. But there is another issue that has also had a great influence—namely, the relation, or lack of one, between the rights that people have in society and in a state of nature.

The Continuity Thesis

(1) In *Anarchy, State, and Utopia* Robert Nozick offers the following hypothetical:

If there were ten Robinson Crusoes, each working alone for two years on separate islands, who discovered each other and the facts of their different allotments by radio communication via transmitters left twenty years earlier, could they not make claims on each other, supposing it were possible to transfer goods from one island to the next? Wouldn't the one with the least make a claim on ground of need, or on the ground that his island was naturally poorest, or on the ground that he was naturally least capable of fending for himself? . . . [S]uch claims clearly would be without merit. Why would they clearly be without merit? In the social noncooperation situation, it might be said, each individual deserves what he gets unaided by his own efforts; or rather, no one else can make a claim *of justice* against this holding. (Nozick, 1974, 185)

In terms of rights Nozick's point is that no Robinson Crusoe has a right to welfare, either on the basis of his needs, or on the basis of any (other) principle of justice, or on any other basis. Nozick's views actually go further in this direction, for he believes that, absent voluntary arrangements, no one has any positive rights against anyone else—at least in a state of nature. This point of view echoes a point made by Judith Thomson, who imagines a situation in which she is "sick unto death," and only the "touch of Henry Fonda's cool hand on [her] fevered brow" will save her life. She maintains that she has no right to Fonda's saving her, even if he is only across the room. (Thomson, 1971, 55) And in her famous violinist case, Thomson says that even if a violinist needs to be plugged into your circulatory system for only one day, he has no right to maintain his life in that way; he would have a right only if you have in some way assumed that responsibility. Absent that, it would be nice if you were to help, but you don't have to. (Thomson, 1971)

Nozick holds that what is true in a state of nature is true also in political society—namely that people's positive rights are determined entirely by their voluntary agreements. So if you have no right to beneficence, welfare, education, or whatever in a state of nature, you have none in society either.

In a section of his book entitled "Macro and Micro" Nozick discusses the relation between how we should think about moral-political principles in relatively simply interpersonal situations and in complex social situations. (Nozick, 1974, 204 ff) Part of his claim is epistemological. He says that in trying to find principles governing human affairs, it is better to find them in relatively simple interpersonal situations, where our intuitions are clearer (or at least his intuitions are clearer), and then apply the principles thus discovered to all situations, however complex. Nozick has been justly criticized regarding this procedure. For one thing, many people do have fairly clear intuitions with respect to certain complex social situations—so for them, at least, a contrary methodology might seem more appropriate, namely, to discover their principles by focusing on those situations and then to apply them to interpersonal and state-of-nature cases.* Second, wherever one's intuitions seem clearer, it seems strange to recommend accepting a principle without even looking to see whether its implications for other situations are at least acceptable.

But though this criticism is fair, there is nevertheless an important point that Nozick is, I believe, making. Earlier in his book Nozick has insisted, in the same vein as classical social contract theory, that government, or the state, can have no greater rights than individuals have in a state of nature; this is one of the implications of saying that the state is not an entity over and above, and distinct from, the group of individuals who are its members. The other side of this, I think, is that individuals can't have greater rights in political society—including rights against the state and its government—than they would have with respect to one another in a state of nature. This seems to me to be what underlies Nozick's macro/micro methodology. To think that people have rights in political society that they don't have in a state of nature—or, put another way, rights against society that they don't have against individuals who are not officials in a society—is to introduce a discontinuity in rights for which there is no basis. Rights are rights, and if people have them at all, they have them always (disregarding, of course, the special ways, if there are any, in which people can lose their rights). So with

*Nozick's Robinson Crusoe example is a state-of-nature case. The state of nature will be discussed in greater detail in Chapter 7.

respect to a right to welfare, if it exists in political society, then it exists in a state of nature; and if it doesn't exist in a state of nature, it doesn't exist in political society either. Our intuitions being as clear as they are (according to Nozick) in state-of-nature situations, the continuity of rights thesis tells us that there is no right to welfare at all.

Out of this comes Nozick's crucial objection to what he calls end-state theories of distributive justice. These are theories in which principles of distributive justice are selected on the basis of the expected outcomes of implementing them in society. We imagine, in terms of the relative holdings of individuals, or of the extent of holdings, what we think a just society would be, and then select principles that are most likely to achieve that outcome. One important thing that is wrong with this, according to Nozick, is that it creates a discontinuity between the moral situations in and out of society. Indeed, discontinuity is virtually inevitable whenever one separates his thinking about rights in society from questions about rights in a state of nature (or rights between individuals apart from social mechanisms), for, freed from that constraint, one is led inevitably to think of how to divide things up in such a way as to achieve some desired end result.

(2) Nozick has presented us with a challenge. He wants an explanation of why the principles that apply between and among individuals in a state of nature should not also be the ones that apply not only between and among individuals in society, but also with respect to an individual's relations with the collective society through its government. It might be useful, as a contretemps, to look briefly at the views of a writer who addresses at least part of this. In his book *Right and Wrong* Charles Fried holds that each individual has a positive right "against those with whom we live in general communities—cities and states . . . to a fair share of that community's scarce resources." (Fried, 1978, 110) However, one's positive right is not to any particular resources, such as education and medical care, but rather to a fair share of the opportunity for obtaining them—that is, to a fair share of money, which is "a generalized claim on the resources of the society as indexed by their scarcity relative to demand." (Fried, 1978, 125)

Fried regards this positive right as grounded in respect for persons, which requires "affirmative care" for others' situations, and a positive contribution to their welfare. "[I]t is inconceivable that respect for common humanity should compel the recognition of the negative rights of our fellow men even at disastrous cost to ourselves, while leaving us totally indifferent to their needs. . . ." (Fried, 1978, 118) But Fried acknowledges that the positive right he has described is "an exclusively institutional concept of positive rights: the obligation is owed to the organized community and the positive rights are claimed from that community. This is not to deny positive rights and duties of beneficence in cases of individual need—the Good Samaritan problem. It is just that once the institutional case is taken care of, the individual case will be much easier to deal with." (Fried, 1978, 119)

As to the Good Samaritan problem, Fried later asks whether we can escape the demands of our common humanity, which is what grounds the positive right to a fair share of a society's resources, "by hiding behind institutions." (Fried, 1978, 130) For there are cases of need not dealt with by institutions. Thomson's example of needing to have Henry Fonda place his cool hand on her fevered brow might be a useful case to think about, as well as the cases Fried is thinking about—cases of need that are anomalous in that they have somehow been missed by the society's distributive institutions. What Fried says about these cases is instructive: " . . . we might recognize a duty to lend assistance without endangering the discretionary space I have been arguing for. By hypothesis the case will be rare. And we may assume that if the institutions are indeed just, devices will obtain for compensating the rescuer after the fact. Thus there is no difficulty about including, as part of the background conditions of just institutions, a set of corresponding rights and duties to relieve immediate, critical and anomalous needs." (Fried, 1978, 130) Concerning what he regards as the more difficult problem of duties to those who are the victims of unjust institutions, Fried says that he has no answer. Our duty is to give our fair share, not to give up everything.

Fried says nothing about rights in a state of nature, but given his constraints on non-institutional rights in society, we must take it that on his view there are far fewer rights, and certainly less imposing rights, in a state of nature than in society. Apparently, then, Fried does not agree with Nozick's continuity of rights thesis. If Nozick's ten Robinson Crusoes formed a society, each individual would, according to Fried, have a right to welfare, or at least a right to a fair share of total resources; but, on Fried's view, as things are a needy Robinson Crusoe has no comparable right on the basis of which he can press a claim against better off Robinson Crusoes.

(3) Both Nozick and Fried think in terms of general rights. Both think that rights are things that people already have, as part, so to speak, of their moral equipment, prior to encountering one another in various conflictual situations. When confronted with such situations, people point to these rights as grounds for their claims to

prevail, and when the weighing and balancing is finished, one of them is seen to have weightier rights and thus to prevail. In cases where one side has a right and the other has none, things are simpler—unless rights can be outweighed by considerations not involving rights.

The difference between Nozick and Fried concerns which rights people have—in particular, whether anyone has a positive right to welfare or to any form of beneficence. Whereas Nozick thinks people never have such rights, Fried thinks that in some broadly characterized types of situations people do have such rights, but not in others. In particular, Fried apparently thinks that in a state of nature people have no right to a fair share of available resources, though perhaps they have some rights to beneficence—at least when it isn't too costly. In society, on the other hand, there is, according to Fried, a right to a fair share, to be made available through social institutions, and with respect to individuals there is a right to beneficence, at least, again, when it isn't too costly.

The question for us to think about here is: if rights are thought of in the way that both Nozick and Fried think of them—as general rights, functioning as above—how can the circumstances (state of nature versus state of society; costly to fulfill versus not too costly to fulfill) determine whether or not people have a given right at all (as opposed to determining whether a right, though possessed, is overridden)?

For one thing, this approach risks running the idea of rights into the ground. It's one thing to say (whatever other difficulties there are in saying it) that in a given situation a person has a (general, prima facie) right which is (or may be) outweighed. But it's quite another thing to say that, because of the circumstances, one has no (general, prima facie) right at all. For if the question whether one has a general right at all is too responsive to circumstances, then such rights don't do any work. The real moral work would have been done in terms of other (non-rights) considerations, and the claim that one should prevail because he or she has a general right would be an afterthought at best, and false at worst. So, at the least, if features of situations are to be relevant in determining whether one has a general right at all, one must be sufficiently non-discriminating among situations and circumstances; one must not permit too many variables to influence whether there is a right at all. These considerations seem to me to rule out questions of cost in determining whether there are general, justificatory rights.

On the other hand, the very presence or absence of a political society—of a government and other social institutions—might not be ruled out by the foregoing considerations. But we must remember that, with respect to many mooted rights, there is, even within political society, the question of whether one has them with respect to individuals or only with respect to the collective society. And so even if one were to decide that the circumstance of whether there is a political society or not is relevant to whether there are certain general rights, for many rights the question will very likely reappear even within the framework of society.

Let us, however, take the broader question—whether the presence or absence of a political society can make a difference to a person's rights. Nozick argues that a state of nature and a state of society are not dissimilar in the relevant respects, so that there is no case for a right to welfare in society that does not exist outside of society. (Nozick, 1974, 185-189) Specifically, what he denies is that "social cooperation introduces a muddying of the waters that makes it unclear or indeterminate who is entitled to what." (Nozick, 1974, 185-186) As important as this matter is, we will leave it aside, for the question presently being raised is how significant differences in social structure (including absence of social structure) could make any difference with respect to rights. Of course, we are speaking only of fairly basic rights. If political structures bring technological advances, and there are rights with respect to these, this is not a telling instance of rights in society that do not exist in a state of nature.

It will be difficult to give a complete answer to the question, for it requires that we look at the bases on which general rights are ascribed, and see whether, on those grounds, it makes a difference whether people are in a state of nature or in society. Fried, for example, grounds the positive right to welfare in respect for persons and in the humanity that is common to us all, binding us together and to one another. (Fried, 1978, 118) But if this grounds rights in society, it should equally ground the same rights outside of society, for all that appears to have changed is the capacity to provide for people's welfare and well-being, not the character of persons or humanity. Indeed, any theory of rights that tries to find the ground of rights in features—such as rationality, autonomy, and uniqueness—inherent in persons will face the difficulty that on such grounds there is no basis for distinguishing people's rights depending on their living in or out of society.

It was not for nothing that classical natural rights theorists tried to find bases for rights in elements of personhood. Given the conception of rights as general justificatory items, and as part of a person's moral equipment, carried about and deployed as needed in a variety of situations, it seems almost evident that they can't be altered by circumstances, inasmuch as they must be capable of doing moral service in a wide variety of circumstances. Perhaps a right can be overridden in certain circumstances, but that is not a case of circumstances altering the very having of the right. If there are, as Thomas Nagel suggests, "principles which give these [i.e., Nozick's] results for small-scale individual transactions but rather different results for the specification of general conditions of entitlement to be applied on an indefinitely larger scale," (Nagel, 1975, 141) one wants to learn what they are. And if one wants, with Thomas Scanlon, to think of natural rights not in the "stronger sense that they are the very same rights which individuals possess and can claim against one another in a state of nature," but instead as representing "general judgments about the conditions of legitimacy of social institutions, for example, judgments of the form 'Any institutions granting *that* power are morally unacceptable' " (Scanlon, 1976, 20) then hasn't one abandoned the theory of general rights?

(4) Scanlon's suggestion, immediately preceding, calls for further comment. Justice, it has sometimes been said, is a property of social institutions. The justice here referred to is distributive justice, and the claim is that the idea of a just distribution has a place only in social life, and that justice is a virtue not of everyone, but of institutions and officials. This is the view of John Rawls in *A Theory of Justice* (1971) and is suggested by Scanlon. If the suggestion is limited to what has just been said, I am not much interested in disagreeing with it. But if the suggestion is broadened so as to include all rights, then I am.

Some writers seem to think that theories of rights and of justice are the same things. But this is not the case. The two are, of course, connected. If there are principles of justice, an individual would probably be said to have a right to what those principles allocate to him. Or one might take the view that justice consists in having one's rights fulfilled. But in the former case principles of justice are only one source of rights, and in the latter a source of rights is still needed.

But if theories of justice and of rights are not the same, then so far there is no ground for thinking that rights exist only within the framework of social institutions. Even if there are some rights that can plausibly be thought of only within social contexts—as some writers think about rights of property—this need not be the case with respect to all rights.

Of course, one could, as many writers seem to do, merely restrict one's thinking to social situations. One could say that he is interested only in the rights of contemporary people in complex industrial and technological societies. This is the tack taken by Ronald Dworkin in *Taking Rights Seriously* (1978) in which he argues for the right to equal concern and respect as the ultimate political right. But it is hard to see how one is to get a comprehensive theory of rights out of this, a theory that includes the rights of individuals with respect to one another apart from social institutions. At this point we are, I think, up against questions of moral methodology which will not be addressed here. For I wish to hold the discussion to attempts to reject the continuity-of-rights thesis that do not rest merely on what amounts to a decision to isolate favored cases for theoretical treatment.

Rights to Beneficence

The continuity thesis seems to be correct. As a consequence, if there are differences between the general, justificatory rights that people are said to have in society and in a state of nature, there must be some telling difference between the two. The usual sorts of attempts, such as Fried's, to provide foundations for such rights do not distinguish between rights in a state of nature and in a social state, thus committing such theorists to more rights than they probably want to acknowledge, and also conflicting with some (perhaps many) people's intuitions. The contentions of the remainder of this chapter are that there can be duties of beneficence in a state of nature, and, indeed, even rights to beneficence; that, via the continuity thesis, such rights can exist in a social state as well; and that there can be such rights not only with respect to acts that a person must perform for another's benefit, but with respect to resources they must provide. On the other hand, while there can be such rights against individuals, it does not follow that there can be rights of a similar sort against the organized society. A case for rights of the latter sort will be presented in chapter 7.

In all of this, a central theme is that once we give up the idea of general, justificatory rights, there seem to be far fewer reservations about rights to beneficence.

(5) First, it will be helpful to discuss the notion of supererogation, for some people might take the view that supererogation means that beneficence is beyond duty, so that if there are duties of beneficence, then there is no place for the supererogatory. After all, if doing good for, or even preventing harm to, others is expected, then what would it be to do more than what is expected.

Let us assume for the moment that there can be duties of beneficence—that sometimes it is not merely that it would be a good thing to do x but that one has an obligation to do something for another even in the absence of some special relation to that other person or some special role or office. Now suppose that N's doing x would save someone M from great harm, but would risk substantial but not as great harm to himself or to others whom N would prefer to save from harm. In such a case, I would say, N has a right not to do x, even though it would be a good thing if he were to do x. And similarly for an act that would be of great benefit to M but would result in N or others whom he would prefer to benefit missing out on some substantial but lesser benefit. So while there might be cases in which there is a duty of beneficence, possible consequences to the agent or to those who he prefers can take a beneficent act out of the class of duties and make it a matter of the agent's prerogative.

All supererogatory acts are of this sort: they are cases of not standing on one's rights when one could do so. Supererogatory acts seem to call for special praise, which one merits not merely for doing the good thing, but for doing so when he has a sufficient moral justification for doing otherwise. On the other hand, if the class of supererogatory acts is the class of acts deserving special praise, then not all cases of not standing on one's rights involve supererogation. Small favors are nonduties—one has a right not to do them, but they don't call for special praise. There is, however, one kind of case, discussed by A. M. Honoré, that appears to count against the idea that supererogatory acts are particularly meritorious cases of not standing on one's rights. This is the case of the individual "who has a professional or quasi-professional duty to undertake rescues." "If the fireman, policeman, or lifesaver risks life or limb to help the imperiled, he deserves and receives praise, because there is an element of self-sacrifice or even heroism in his conduct, though what he does is clearly his duty. Heroism and self-sacrifice, unlike altruism, can be evinced both by those who do their duty and those who have no duty to do." (Honoré, 1966, 230) Now certainly a person can have a duty to take risks, and one who has such a duty can be especially praiseworthy for the risks he takes. But equally certainly even a person who has a duty to take risks is not required to take any and every risk—even a professional rescuer can risk more than duty requires. It seems to me that though some sort of congratulations is fitting for taking risks required by duty, this is at the most an expression of admiration at someone's being able and willing to take risks at all, and is not the same as the special praise reserved for those who don't hold back when they would be justified in so doing—though this special praise is itself often mixed with the sort of admiration, just referred to, at another's willingness to take any risks at all.

(6) Are there duties of beneficence? Many people take the view that there are duties to come forward for the sake of those to whom we stand in special relationships, but not for others. A parent is expected to aid his or her child, and a husband is expected to aid his wife, and vice versa. Some find it easy to extend this to lovers and friends, and to those with whom we are engaged in common enterprises.

The question, we must remember, is not whether it would be a good thing, in these cases, to come forward for the benefit of others, or whether one ought to do so, but whether one must, morally speaking, do so. Consider the following case, which is intuitively a strong case for there being duties of beneficence. Suppose that a small child is drowning in shallow water, and that Jones, the only person standing nearby, could easily save the child with little inconvenience to himself and only modest effort. Part of the resistance of some to the idea that Jones has an obligation here seems to come from the sense that Jones has no responsibility for that child, since one acquires a responsibility for someone else only by *taking* responsibility. There might also be connected with this the sense that obligations are burdens and that it is in some way unfair to be stuck with such a burden entirely fortuitously—merely by being in the right place at the right time (or the wrong place at the wrong time). Again the resistance seems to be to the idea that one can get stuck with the burden of obligation without having voluntarily done anything to take it on.

But the notion of taking responsibility for something is tricky. Does a person take responsibility for some eventuality e only if he explicitly assumes responsibility for eventualities like e, should they occur, or does he instead take responsibility for eventualities like e if he undertakes an enterprise knowing that e might occur (or even, sometimes, if he doesn't know that e might occur)? For example, one who has a child takes responsibility for its safety; one can't disclaim responsibility by saying "I will feed and house this child, but will do nothing to insure its safety; if it is drowning, I assume no responsibility for doing anything about it." So if it is Jones's child drowning in the pond he has an obligation to save it irrespective of an explicit assumption of responsibility. How is the case different if it isn't Jones's child? Jones merely walks by the pond (aware that sometimes people drown). True, the cases aren't exactly alike, morally speaking. One must take greater risks for his own child; and if one's own child and a stranger's child are both drowning it might be obligatory to save one's own first. But if one can be obligated to save his own child without an explicit assumption of responsibility, then at least there can be no conclusive objection to the claim that Jones has an obligation of beneficence, merely on the ground that he hasn't explicitly assumed an obligation.

But, someone might say, there is still all the difference between the cases—after all, in one there is a relationship between the parties, but not in the other, and that relationship grounds the moral requirement that one act to prevent harm to the other. Now it is easy to agree with most of this, but one wants to know exactly why, and how, the existence of the relationship grounds a moral requirement in one case, whereas there is said to be no moral requirement whatsoever in circumstances that are identical except for the relationship. As before, it's not a matter of a voluntary undertaking. Someone might argue that it is indeed a matter of voluntary undertaking, in that there are obligations built into certain relationships, and anyone who voluntarily enters into such a relationship thereby voluntarily undertakes the obligations that are part of it. But this will not do, for the very question is whether these obligations are built in, and how they got built in. Are they built into the relationships of lovers? friends? acquaintances? How can we tell?

Pretty clearly the question of whether there are moral requirements in cases of special relationships can't be answered in terms of voluntary undertakings, but even more clearly there must be principles for moral judgment in such cases. How we go about trying to find or develop such principles is, of course, a large question—which is the topic of chapter 6. My own view on the case being discussed here is that there is clearly a moral requirement with respect to one's children (I assume that everyone agrees with this), and that appropriate moral principles don't distinguish so sharply between family, intimates, and strangers that there could never be a case in which one has a duty of beneficence where the beneficiary is a stranger.

(7) A person can have a right to do what he ought not to do (what it would be a good thing if he were not to do), or a right not to do what he ought to do. Cases of "just being nice" and of doing favors are obvious examples. Judith Thomson's examples are again useful. One has a right, she says, to bury his ice cream in the garden rather than give it to someone else who would like to have it. But what if the ice cream is needed by another person to stave off starvation? According to Thomson, the owner still has the right to bury it in the garden. And she says that if she were sick unto death and only the cool hand of Henry Fonda on her fevered brow would save her, Henry Fonda would have the right not to cross the country or even the room to save her life. Thomson's views here seem to derive from a particular conception of rights: how, she apparently thinks, could

one have a property right, or a right to liberty, or any other kind of right, if the above were not implications of having these rights? On the conception of rights developed in this book, however, the foregoing are not consequences; we do not argue from the having of a (general) right to one's particular rights in concrete circumstances; rather, we ask whether the relevant moral considerations in each particular case support the claim that someone actually has a right to do or to have something—i.e., a sufficient justification for exercising his prerogative in the circumstances. So at least as far as the concept of rights is concerned, the question of whether there are rights in the examples might depend on how bad it will be for others if I bury the ice cream or if Henry Fonda doesn't place his cool hand on Professor Thomson's fevered brow. Thus do we avoid the "shocking idea that anyone's rights should fade away and disappear as it gets harder and harder to accord them. . . ." (Thomson, 1971, 61)

Is there ever a right to beneficence? It would be a mistake to say that obligations entail rights, so that where there is a duty of beneficence there is a right of the beneficiary to the benefaction. For there are cases in which there are duties but no corresponding rights—as in the case of what Feinberg calls duties of obedience. (Feinberg, 1966, 141-142) When a policeman, acting within his authority, orders me to do something, I have a duty to do it, but neither the policeman nor anyone else thereby has a personal right to my doing it. Still, it could be argued, if, on a particular occasion, N has a duty to save M, isn't the duty owed to M? And if so, can it be denied that M has a right to N's saving him? Perhaps not, if, in having a duty to save M, N really owes that duty to M. But it has not been established that in having a duty to do something for the benefit of another, one has (owes) a duty *to* that other person. Even in the clearest case of owing—the owing of money—what one owes to another is money, not a duty. One has a duty to pay money he owes; the money, not the duty, is what is owed.

Nevertheless, there seems to be little reason to deny that there can be a right to beneficence if there can be a duty of beneficence. For if, morally speaking, N has to save M, there can hardly be any objection to holding that M is justified in insisting that N save him. In saying that N has an obligation we have already said that it is not merely that he ought to save M, that it would be a good thing if he were to do so. We are saying, rather, that there are reasons why N must do so; these same reasons would (probably) justify M in insisting on it. After all, it is not as if N has the obligation only *because* M has a right that he insists on.

It should be noted that even in some cases of the foregoing sort we can still make sense of the idea that in having a right one has a justification for insisting on certain behavior in the face of reasons against so doing. If N had, say, a duty to prevent M from starving, or to take care of his (N's) invalid parent P, it might be the case that both M and P would be justified in insisting on N's doing the appropriate thing, but that neither of them ought to do so. M, perhaps, ought not to impose himself on others, particularly where so doing would require a sacrifice of N's welfare; it might be a good thing if M were to try to help himself and to suffer the worst if he can't. And likewise it might be that P ought not to create serious problems in his child's life and in his family relations.

So far it has been assumed that the moral considerations that establish a duty of beneficence on a particular occasion also establish a justification for the beneficiary's insisting on it. But this may not be so in all cases. It seems plausible that there could be cases in which N has a duty of beneficence but M has no right to it. Suppose, for example, that N will be put to some small but tangible expense or loss in rescuing M, and that M, though he could do so, has no intention of compensating N for these losses. M might then not be justified in insisting on N's beneficence, even though N may still have a duty to rescue. N's costs might not be sufficiently great to make his behavior a matter of his prerogative, but might neverthe-less undermine M's moral position. When it comes to rights there is a kind of "clean hands" notion, familiar in the law of equity: he who has morally unclean hands lacks standing to press his claim, even if, on the merits of the case, he has a good claim.

(8) The United Nations Universal Declaration of Human Rights states that everyone has, among other things, the right to work, the right to food, to housing, to medical care, and to education. Rights of this sort are sometimes called social and economic rights, and are distinguished from political and civil rights such as those referred to in the United States Declaration of Independence and Constitution, and in similar documents. Rights of this sort have been called rights of recipience, which category includes such rights as rights to health, food, essential medical and hospital care, and higher education.

One worry about the right to some resource is how there can be such a right when there isn't any of the resource—i.e., "when the right physically cannot fully or even partially be acknowl-edged. . . ." (McCloskey, 1978, 106) This worry, it seems to me, is readily dealt with by the account of rights presented in this book. For there is no general right to some resource or state of affairs; there is a right only when, in the full circumstances, one would be justified in insisting on something, and if there is no x, there can be no justifiable insistence on x. Furthermore, to speak of a right-to-x (as, a right to food) without referring to a particular resource or state of affairs seems to do no more than to say that some interests are particularly important and morally relevant. The language of rights is not needed for this; the terminology of needs and interests is sufficient for that purpose; rights terminology has a different role. But though there is no general right to resources or states of affairs, a person may have a right, in some circumstances, to another person's making efforts to make needed resources available. This might take the form of a right to a change in certain institutional structures, so that needed resources might be available in the future.

There is another aspect of right-to-x claims that remains to be discussed. Such claims often assert rights to such things as food, education, and health care—i.e., to resources. Much of the resistance to claims of social and economic rights concerns the suggestion that one person could have a right to another's giving him something that hasn't been earned or paid for, where there is no special relation between the individuals.

If there is ever a right to beneficence there is no reason, in principle, why there couldn't be a right to be provided resources by another. We have suggested before that N might have a duty to save M from drowning even if M must bear some small losses or expenses; and though M's having a right to be saved by N might depend on his willingness to compensate N for his losses, M might still have a right to be saved by N even if he can't compensate him. But if this is so it would seem that there could be cases, in which the resources themselves are desperately needed, in which M can't compensate N, and in which M nevertheless has a right to the resources.

Two comments can be offered in explanation of why there is great resistance to the idea that there can be a right to be provided resources by others. First, part of the resistance goes to the difference between doing some act or performing some service for another, and giving another person one's resources. The difference is that whereas usually one's time and physical exertions are easily replaced, most people's resources are less easily replaced. Many people, having provided resources for themselves, would much rather use their spare time to assist others than give up some of their resources, even if they can spare the resources. This being the case, we should not be surprised to find that stronger cases can be made for rights to beneficial services than for rights to resources.

The second worry is that if M has a moral right to N's doing something such as saving him from drowning or providing needed resources, then the law ought to protect that right by forcing N to save M or to provide him with resources. The thought here seems to be that even if N has a duty in these cases, so long as it is only a moral duty it is up to him whether or not to fulfill it, whereas if the law enforces it it is no longer up to his conscience alone. In mitigation of this it can be pointed out that not all rights ought to be legally protected, due (at least in part) to the external costs of legal enforcement. But this only mitigates; it does not show that there could not be cases in which a right to be provided services or resources by another should be legally protected.

Issues concerning the legitimacy of legally enforcing certain kinds of behavior are quite complex in a majoritarian political system tempered by constitutional limitations, but, these aside, the question is whether a right to resources implies that one might legitimately be forced, by penal sanction or civil redress (for example, by being sued for failing to rescue), to provide services or resources. It seems very likely that a right to resources would sometimes warrant legal protection of such a right. (See chapter 8.) We should not, however, assume too quickly that the fact that there can be rights to be provided resources, and that such rights might be legally recognized, make a case for government instituting a tax supported welfare system so as to obviate the need for individuals to provide resources directly, such that one person's right to another's providing resources thus becomes a right to the government's providing resources. As we shall see in chapter 7, rights against the collective society rest on an entirely different ground from rights against individuals.

6

Intuitionism

In chapters 7 and 8 we will take up further matters that require reaching conclusions about the rights that people have. Arguments must be given, and judgments made, and to this end some sort of moral theory is needed. We should not be surprised to find, however, that an ethicist's ideas about right and wrong and other moral categories might depend in part on ideas about what the structure of an adequate moral theory should be. The purpose of this chapter is, accordingly, to examine certain views about what an adequate moral theory must be like, so as to clear the way for the discussions in the succeeding chapters.

One of the most significant differences among moral theories is that between monistic and pluralistic theories. The difference is better shown than explained, and will become apparent as some ideas about the adequacy of moral theories are examined in what follows. A good place to begin is with W. D. Ross's pluralistic theory. (Ross, 1930)

Ross thinks of a moral theory as consisting of a set of rules, which are to be applied to the circumstances of concrete cases to determine what one is obligated to do or refrain from doing. Ross must, of course, deal with the possibility of exceptions to rules, and also explain how conflicts between rules are to be resolved. Rules cannot be made complex enough (i.e., contain enough exceptive clauses) to deal with all of the cases that will arise. But neither can a firm ranking of the rules be given, such that whenever there is a conflict between two rules one of them prevails over the other. Ross avoids these difficulties by thinking in terms of rules of prima facie duty, of which he identifies seven, among which are the rule that one has a prima facie duty to keep promises (the duty of fidelity) and the rule that one has a prima facie duty not to harm others (the duty of non-maleficence). These rules are themselves exceptionless, but they do not prevail in all of the cases in which they are applicable, for any of them can be outweighed, in a given instance, by another. There are, however, no rules determining priorities in concrete cases. It might be the case that one rule will generally outweigh another, but it need not, and one can decide which is to prevail only by some sort of weighing.

Philosophers have never found Ross's notion of a prima facie duty entirely clear or satisfactory. To say that something is a prima facie duty, according to Ross, is not to say that it is merely presumed to be a duty, but neither is it to say that it is a "duty proper"—that is, an actual duty in the circumstances. Rather, it is to say that a certain act is a "duty proper" unless there are other prima facie duties outweighing it. This explanation of a prima facie duty risks being circular, for "duty proper" can be defined only in terms of the notion of prima facie duty. So the question of what a prima facie duty is has not adequately been explained, and Ross complicates the problem by holding that being a prima facie duty is a property of an act, without saying exactly what that property is which my owing you money and my lack of intelligence (which gives rise to a prima facie duty of self-improvement) have in common.

An Objection

While I do not want to discuss all of the objections that have been raised in connection with Ross's theory, there is an important objection that I do want to consider, a useful presentation of which is found in a recent textbook on ethics. Ross's theory consists of a set of prima facie rules. But of course it is crucial to be able to determine, on the basis of these rules, one's actual obligation in concrete situations. Ross's rules are not absolute (i.e., categorical), but neither is there a hierarchy of rules in which some rule is always stronger than some other rule—for in some circumstances one rule might be stronger than another, whereas in other circumstances the reverse might be true. But, then,

Since the two rules of morality are not being used to determine which of the two conflicting rules of morality overrides the other, what basis do we have for making such a determination? . . . What we seem to use . . . is the knowledge that in this set of circumstances one of the proposed actions is obligatory and the other is not. However, if we can determine without the use of prima facie rules that one action is obligatory and the other is not, then the rules cannot be the complete explanation of how to arrive at justified moral judgments. The basis of justified moral judgments cannot be the set of prima facie rules because we have at hand at least some justified moral judgments that are arrived at without the use of the rules. This conclusion, of course, is completely incompatible with a prima facie rule theory. (Rosen, 1978, 127)

Can Ross's theory be beefed up by adding more rules—secondary, or meta-moral, or indirect—rules that settle conflicts by telling us which of two conflicting prima facie rules overrides the other—not in all cases, but in certain sorts of situations? This rule must itself be a prima facie rule, for even in a given *sort* of situation circumstances might be such that a different ordering of primary rules prevails. The objection then continues:

If something is a prima facie indirect moral rule, though, there has to be at least one other such rule—for there is no such thing as one prima facie rule of anything. However, if there are at least two such indirect prima facie rules, then there will, again, be a situation in which there is a conflict of those two. And now the same problem arises that arose at the beginning: the conflict of the two indirect prima facie rules is either to be settled with the aid of a rule or without it. As we have seen, it is not possible for a prima facie rule theorist to allow the conflict to be settled without the aid of a rule. Therefore, the rule must be either a prima facie rule or a categorical rule. However, as we have already established it cannot be a categorical rule. Thus it must be a prima facie rule. However, it cannot be an indirect rule of the same type as the two that conflict, or else it could not settle the conflict. If it is of a different level, then there is at least one other prima facie rule at that level with which *it* can conflict, and the conflict problem has not yet been resolved. . . . Thus we see that the conflict situation leads forever to other conflict situations—something philosophers call a *vicious infinite regress.* (Rosen, 1978, 130-131)

A Modification of Ross

As indicated previously, Ross has a good deal of difficulty explaining exactly what a prima facie duty is, and some commentators have come to the conclusion that it is not a coherent notion. From the standpoint of moral pluralism, however, that notion is not necessary. We can think instead of a morality consisting of a group of principles identifying certain matters (for examples, consequences of acts and of kinds of acts, relations among individuals, and the character of individuals performing acts, among others) as having moral relevance, perhaps with some suggestion as to their degree of importance. Not all of these are principles of duty, though. Some might refer only to values, virtues, and other matters. Now this certainly seems a far cry from Ross's conception of morality as a set of principles concerning duty, though the difference is not that great. For, like Ross's set of prima facie duties, this grab-bag of principles is oriented toward how people should (often, indeed, have a moral duty to) behave; it differs from Ross in that not each element in the grab-bag is itself a principle referring explicitly to some duty. But for our purposes the grab-bag of principles is importantly like Ross's ethical theory in that it too requires weighing and balancing in deciding what one is morally required (or whatever) to do in concrete cases. And, of course, the objections raised above may be equally applicable.

Just to be clear that we have the proper focus, it would be well to point out that these principles are not just exceptionless rules. There are two ways in which rules can have exceptions. There can be exceptions to a rule, in which case the rule is not applied at all, or there can be exceptive clauses as *part of* a rule, in which case the rule *is* being applied when the exceptive clause is applicable. For example, legitimately going 60 mph in a 30 mph zone would be an exception to the rule "The maximum permissible speed is 30 mph," but would be an application of the rule "The maximum permissible speed is 30 mph unless there is an emergency, in which case whatever speed is reasonably compatible with traffic conditions is permissible." Now one might think that so-called principles are just rules awaiting their exceptive clauses, and that once these are added, there will be no need for weighing and balancing. But this would be in error, for principles function in a rather different way. (Dworkin, 1978, 22-28) Let us take as examples the rule in the game Monopoly that the banker must pay $200 from the bank to a player who passes Go, and the principle in our legal system that no one is to profit from his own wrongdoing. The rule sets out the conditions in which it applies, and if those conditions are met, then things must happen as the rule specifies. And it can't be altered or mitigated by circumstances—either it applies with full force, or not at all. A principle, on the other hand, does not set out any specific conditions in which it applies. In a sense it always applies, in that it is applicable in any situation in which there is wrongdoing. But it is not the case that its being applicable means that things can't legitimately turn out contrary to it—for it can exist with full force and yet be outweighed in some cases. Principles, unlike rules, have a dimension of weight, or importance. Principles, then, are not merely rules awaiting exceptive clauses. They are considerations that argue in favor of or against certain actions or policies, and when they do not prevail they are outweighed without being overruled or needing to be modified. What we are examining in this chapter are objections to this way of moralizing, one of which we have already seen.

Alternatives to Intuitionism

By an alternative to intuitionism I mean a way of dealing with or avoiding conflicts without being a pluralist-intuitionist. One way to avoid intuitionism is to find principles that rationalize the intuitionist's assignments of weights. Thus Rawls: "Of course, it may be claimed that in the assignment of weights we are guided, without being aware of it, by certain further standards or by how best to realize a certain end. Perhaps the weights we assign are those which would result if we were to apply these standards or to pursue this end." (Rawls, 1971, 39) This amounts, I believe, to the suggestion that the intuitionist's moral theory is not what he says or even thinks it is. Rather, there are other considerations that are being appealed to in order to settle conflicts among principles, and it is these considerations that either constitute, or are at least a necessary and significant part of, the intuitionist's moral theory. Intuitionists, according to Rawls, deny this.

Admittedly any given balancing of principles is subject to interpretation in this way. But the intuitionist claims that, in fact, there is no such interpretation. He contends that there exists no expressible ethical conception which underlies these weights. A geometrical figure or a mathematical function may describe them, but there are no constructive moral criteria that establish their reasonableness. Intuitionism holds that in our judgments of social justice we must eventually reach a plurality of first principles in regard to which we can only say that it seems to us more correct to balance them this way rather than that. (Rawls, 1971, 39)

We will return to this line of thought later.

Another way to avoid intuitionism, of course, is to reject pluralism—to deny, that is, that there are a number of first principles which can only be balanced in concrete cases, where there are no principles governing—or better, determining—the way the balancing is to come out. Simple utilitarianism is a theory of this sort. Think of the version in which a person is always to do that act which will lead to at least as favorable a balance of pleasure over pain as any other available alternative. On such a theory all acts can, in principle, be ranked in terms of a single standard, and there is no problem of having to balance moral values. This feature alone has made utilitarianism very attractive to a great many people, and proponents of more complex varieties of utilitarianism find it necessary to struggle to hold on to this ordering property of utilitarianism, and think of the possible failure of utilitarianism in this respect as a decided defect in the theory. More will be said about utilitarianism further on.

Alternatives to Intuitionism: Blind Alleys

At this point I would like to consider some other lines of thought connected with the problem of conflicts among moral principles. These lines of thought have been developed in connection with what in the literature is being called a coherence approach to morality. (See Dworkin, 1978, 159-168.) The idea is akin to a pragmatic approach to knowledge. A person has beliefs about the rightness or wrongness of particular acts in concrete situations, and perhaps also beliefs about general moral principles. The task is to be sure that all of these cohere in a consistent system. Suppose I were to find that some of my particular moral judgments were not consistent with some moral principle that I believe. Then I must either modify the principle, or abandon it altogether, or else abandon or alter those particular moral judgments. Likewise, if I find that I have a group of particular moral judgments, I must ask what general moral principle organizes them, showing that they are consistent with one another and that they cohere intelligently. If I don't have satisfactory answers to these questions, I must change things until I do, and anything in the package—the principle or the particular judgments—can be changed. As Rawls puts it, I can work from both ends, adjusting either or both the principles and the particular judgments until I get a coherent set that I can accept. (Rawls, 1971, 20)

There are two significant elements in the coherence approach. First, moral judgments and principles are not taken to be descriptive of a moral reality, so that, in fashioning a coherent moral theory, one is neither discovering nor rejecting an independent truth. And second, one is, accordingly, free to reject moral beliefs (including some that seem intuitively clear) as one wishes, toward the end of producing a coherent set of beliefs.

The most influential ethical theory devised to date by a coherence methodology is Rawls's. It will be useful to work backwards, first looking at the substantive outcome of Rawls's meta-theory, and then at the lines of thought leading to that outcome. Rawls's two principles of justice are:

First, each person is to have an equal right to the most extensive basic liberty compatible with a similar liberty for others.

Second, social and economic inequalities are to be arranged so that they are both (a) reasonably expected to be to everyone's advantage, and (b) attached to positions and offices open to all. (Rawls, 1971, 60)

These principles are not, for Rawls, all there is to morality—there are other principles, of fairness and of natural duty. But the two principles are the central element in Rawls's morality, for they define social justice—i.e., justice with respect to roles and office in society, basic human needs, and freedom. These form a moral core, and many of the other concerns of a full and adequate morality can be expressed with reference to this core. What is of particular importance for our purposes is that the two principles are in what Rawls calls serial or lexical order—the first must, if applicable, be satisfied before the second comes into play. And this avoids any problem—what Rawls calls the priority problem—of having to balance competing principles: "a serial ordering avoids . . . having to balance principles at all; those earlier in the ordering have an absolute weight, so to speak, with respect to later ones, and hold without exception." (Rawls, 1971, 43)

There are in Rawls two arguments for (or lines of thought leading to) lexical order. One is a straightforward argument employing the coherence approach to morality, Rawls's version of which he calls the technique of reflective equilibrium, and the other is an argument to the effect that people in a certain choice situation would, on the basis of rational self-interest, select the two principles in lexical order.

Let us start by looking at the second—the contract—argument. Rawls asks us to imagine a group of people having to choose principles for the structure of the social institutions under which they will live, but having no reasonable way of determining in advance how they would fare when the principles to be selected come to be put into effect. Rawls believes that people who were behind a "veil of ignorance," knowing nothing specific about their talents and level of intelligence, background, race, sex, education and whatever else might lead a person to prefer principles that favored people having such characteristics, would individually and collectively settle on the two principles for the governance of their lives in society. For the first principle treats everyone the same— granting equal liberty to everyone—and so favors no one at others' expense. And though the second principle permits social differ- ences, everyone can agree to accept it because it permits the society as a whole to be better off without penalizing anyone unacceptably. The argument for, and operation of, the second principle (the "difference" principle) is a bit more complex, but need not detain us here.

Why would the people in this choice situation choose to order the two principles lexically, rather than allow balancing when concrete situations seem to require trade-offs between liberty and welfare (one person's liberty and the same person's or another person's welfare)? Rawls says: "being rational, the persons in the original position recognize that they should consider the priority of these principles. For if they wish to establish agreed standards for adjudicating their claims on one another, they will need principles for assigning weights. They cannot assume that their intuitive judgments of priority will be the same. . . . Thus I suppose that in the original position the parties try to reach some agreement as to how the principles of justice are to be balanced." (Rawls, 1971, 42) This is hardly convincing. Why wouldn't rationally self-interested people establish institutions whose officials would try to identify kinds of cases in which most people *could* agree as to which principle (or value) should prevail? And for other cases mightn't they want their institutions to honor each value some of the time, perhaps shifting back and forth over time, and working out so that no one's intuitions would be consistently overridden? What principle of rationality can demonstrate that it's better to settle once and for all which values or principles are to prevail? Do the people in the original position know something that we don't know—that the sorts of institutions just described can't, or are even unlikely to, work out satisfactorily?

In any event, there is something disquieting about the idea that these questions are to be settled by such crude "pragmatic" considerations rather than moral considerations, and this takes us to the role of reflective equilibrium. The idea, as described earlier, is to find the set of principles and their weights that is in reflective equilibrium with one's considered intuitions; for Rawls himself, the two principles cohere best with his considered intuitions. Intuitions thus have a very important place in moral theory, according to Rawls, and what we want to notice now is exactly what sort of place they have. In Rawls's view, intuitions are relevant for deciding what moral theory to accept, but are out of place within the body of the theory itself. They are part of our moral methodology, but not part of our morality. How does Rawls get to this way of looking at things?

We should note that it is not the very character of a coherence approach to morality that requires avoidance of intuitions within the body of an ethical theory—someone else could, after all, come to the conclusion that the moral principles best capturing the intuitions that he most cares about are multiple and unordered, such that decisions in concrete areas (or some of them anyway) can be made only by appeals to intuition. All that Rawls shows is that his particular intuitions are such that the most favored subset of them coheres best with principles ordered serially.

Here it is important to note a significant difference between the reflective equilibrium argument and the original position argument. In the latter the reasoning must be the same for all, since everyone in the original position is in identical circumstances and rationality is (arguably) the same for all. But not so with respect to the former line of thought, for intuitions differ, both in content and strength. It is unfortunately too easy to run Rawls's two lines of thought together, and some of Rawls's own language encourages this.* Whereas the argument from the original position is entirely prudential, and the argument using the technique of reflective equilibrium a kind of moral argument, one is sometimes led to think of the people in the original position as being engaged in some sort of moral enterprise in which they are to agree on moral principles which are in reflective equilibrium with a subset of the intuitions of all of them, and in which they make compromises in order to reach agreement. If this were what was going on—if people were up to making moral compromises because they were convinced of the importance of coming up with principles they could collectively live with—the case for serial ordering (more precisely, the case for principles that decide concrete cases without the need for recourse to intuitions) might be more convincing, though even here it would not be compelling. But this is not even Rawls's argument. Reflective equilibrium is a one person affair—I can find principles that are in reflective equilibrium with my intuitions, and you can find principles in reflective equilibrium with yours, and they may be different principles. If we choose to get together to try to convince one another, we may come up with principles which both of us accept as being in reflective equilibrium with our newly and jointly considered intuitions, and what two may do, all may do. But we may fail. Or, indeed, we may find that the principles we come up with are multiple and unordered, requiring moral balancing and political uneasiness. There is no basis in Rawls's argument for the idea that the acceptability of an ethical theory depends on an adequate respect being given to (almost) everyone's basic moral intuitions.

There is another sort of idea, very much at home in a coherence

---

*"If men's intuitive priority judgments are similar, it does not matter, practically speaking, that they cannot formulate the principles which account for these convictions, or even whether such principles exist. Contrary judgments, however, raise a difficulty, since the basis for adjudicating claims is to that extent obscure. Thus our object should be to formulate a conception of justice which, however much it may call upon intuition, ethical or prudential, tends to make our considered judgments of justice converge. If such a conception does exist, then, from the standpoint of the original position, there would be strong reasons for accepting it, since it is rational to introduce further coherence into our common convictions of justice. . . . The original agreement settles how far they are prepared to compromise and to simplify in order to establish the priority rules necessary for a common conception of justice." (Rawls, 1971, 45) Compromise *what*?

framework, which offers a way of avoiding intuitionistic pluralism. This idea is suggested by Ronald Dworkin in *Taking Rights Seriously*, and though Dworkin is concerned specifically with political theories, his remarks would apply equally to moral theory generally. "Political theories will differ from one another, therefore, not simply in the particular goals, rights, and duties each set out, but also in the way each connects the goals, rights, and duties it employs. In a well-formed theory some consistent set of these, internally ranked or weighted, will be taken as fundamental or ultimate within the theory." (Dworkin, 1978, 171) Here we are to direct our attention to the notion of a well-formed ethical theory, which is described in such a way that an intuitionistic (pluralistic) theory cannot be well-formed.

Dworkin goes on to say that "it seems reasonable to suppose that any particular theory will give ultimate pride of place to just one of these concepts; it will take some overriding goal, or some set of fundamental rights, or some set of transcendent duties, as fundamental, and show other goals, rights, and duties as subordinate and derivative." (Dworkin, 1971, 171) A theory can be either goal-based, right-based, or duty-based—that is, take as fundamental some goal like improvement of the general welfare, or some right like the right of all men to the greatest possible overall liberty, or some duty like the duty to obey God's will as set forth in the Ten Commandments. A theory having one of these concepts at its heart is likely to be committed to a particular type of ultimate concern: a goal-based theory is ultimately concerned with particular individuals only in so far as such concern advances some general state of affairs; a duty-based theory is concerned with the moral quality of people's acts and the virtues of being a moral person; a right-based theory is concerned with a person's individuality and independence and with the benefits he is entitled to derive from others' behavior.

Now it is clear that Dworkin thinks that it is something like a condition of adequacy for a moral theory that it be well-formed— that it have as a fundamental core a ranked or weighted set of rights, goals, and duties, and preferably limited to just one of these concepts (rights, goals, or duties). Why is this? One reason we can glean from Dworkin is found in his suggestion that taking different moral concepts (rights, duties, goals) as fundamental puts people in different lights: in a duty-based theory a person is seen as one who is to conform, whereas in a right-based theory the independence of individual action is the most significant matter, and a goal-based theory sees the individual merely as a possible locus for the advancement of some larger goal. But even if all of this is correct, it does not tell us why people must ultimately be seen in only one light.

The other reason we can gain from Dworkin is more to the point; it is that an ethical theory without a fundamental core either is, or leads to, incoherence and inconsistency. Of course, from this standpoint one of Dworkin's own examples of an ethical theory with a fundamental concept—the duty to obey God's will as set forth in the Ten Commandments—is hardly a model. But there is indeed a serious problem here—how an ethical theory is to deal with (apparent, at any rate) inconsistencies.

At this point we would do well to examine more carefully a fairly detailed fragment of a possible intuitionistic approach, so as to see precisely what it is that anti-intuitionists object to.

An Intuitionistic Approach

Let us think in terms of a set of general principles. The question is: how, when principles conflict, do they lead to particular judgments in concrete cases? Since conflicts among general principles are so common, particularly in the morally most difficult cases, this problem cannot be regarded by intuitionists as peripheral; it is a central and crucial matter. The difficulty is that insofar as these principles are supposed to be ultimate, and insofar as they do not say which is to prevail when there are conflicts, there are no "rules" for applying them, and thus the ethical theory is indeterminate or inconsistent.

The character of intuitionistic reasoning is no mystery (though it may be a mystery how some people come up with the particular results they do). Everyone is familiar with such reasoning in the area of nonmoral evaluation where there is more than one criterion involved. Suppose I must decide whether k_1 or k_2 is a better knife. Now I happen (we will suppose) to think that there are two things to look at in judging knives—their efficiency in cutting, and their attractiveness. What I will do, then, is rank k_1 and k_2 in terms of their efficiency in cutting, and, separately, in terms of their attractiveness. Suppose it comes out like this:

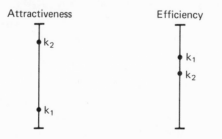

I might then say that k_2 ranks higher in relative attractiveness than k_1 does in efficiency, and judge k_2 the better knife.

Even limited to the same criteria my mode of evaluation might be somewhat more complex. I might, for example, think that efficiency rankings are perfectly linear, so that although in the following

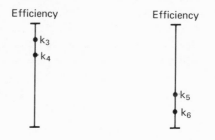

k_3 is as much more efficient than k_4 as k_5 is than k_6, my attractiveness rankings might be something like logarithmic, so that, in the following

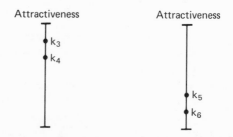

k_3 is *much* more attractive relative to k_4 than k_5 is relative to k_6. Thus, not only the relative rankings of k_1 and k_2 with respect to efficiency and attractiveness determine my final judgment, but their places on these scales might also have an impact.

Something quite similar, though more complex, goes on with respect to intuitionistic reasoning involving moral principles. Let's consider a fragment of a possible intuitionistic theory, dealing with a case in which keeping a promise to someone would cause hurt to others. Imagine someone—say, me—who has the following two principles: Don't hurt people (the principle of non-maleficence), and don't break promises (the principle of promise-keeping). Now suppose this fragment is filled out as follows. Not only can hurts differ in degree, they can also be of different kinds—for example, physical, psychological, emotional. I'm not perfectly clear as to the boundaries of each of these, but I have general ideas, and I have different ideas as to the seriousness of each sort of hurt. Similarly with promises: I identify different (overlapping) sorts of promises, and have different ideas as to the importance of each. Promises can be given seriously or offhandedly; they can be gratuitous or solicited; they can be unilateral or bilateral; they can vary in the degree of reliance that may be placed on them.

Now in a situation in which the principle of promise-keeping comes into conflict with the principle of non-maleficence, I consult the ideas I have about the different sorts of promises. For each type and degree of hurt, I might come up with different results as the character of the promise changes. I might, for example, rate the solemnity of a promise very high, and hold that a very solemn promise outweighs a certain degree of emotional hurt—though I might not allow that it outweighs a comparable degree of physical hurt. I might regard a gratuitous and offhand promise as outweighing small hurts of all sorts if it is bilateral, but as outweighing only small emotional hurts if it is unilateral. And so forth.

Some of my weightings might be such that I can state my attitude in the form of a rule, or as a rule involving certain statable exceptions. In other cases things might be too complex for such a statement—partly because, with respect to some matters, I might have unarticulated attitudes that might exist only as dispositions to make certain judgments when appropriate situations occur. But though I can't state how all of these complicated weighings work out, they can be consistent, and if they aren't, I can and will make alterations to make them consistent. Even if they are consistent, I can alter them—someone may convince me that my categories or priorities are inappropriate, and lead me to modify them.

This, as I understand it, is intuitionism. Whether or not it is exactly what any identifiable writer has meant by it, it's plausible, and it is something we are quite familiar and even comfortable with. And I think that exhibiting the character of intuitionistic thinking answers one of the objections raised against it. Recall that one objection was that sometimes one principle prevails and sometimes another one prevails, without there being any basis for this other than "seeing" in a concrete situation that one of them is weightier. Part of the answer to this is that the intuitionist does not really have *a* principle of non-maleficence and *a* principle of promise-keeping. There are really a large number of principles with respect to both of these, each of them already containing relative weights. Moral reasoning at this level does not, then, consist in applying those very general principles to circumstances; it is rather a matter of identifying—or even constructing—a more specialized principle that refers to the relevant features of the situation and says which are weightier. The intuitionist's theory, then, is not fully statable—not even close to that. The most general principles are in no sense constitutive of the intuitionist's morality; they essentially summarize the areas in which the intuitionist has more refined principles. These "more refined" principles, on the other hand, cannot always (or even often) be stated completely—there are far too many of them and they are too complex. And many of them will never have been articulated—certain sorts of situations may never have been confronted, even in imagination, before, and though you may guess what weighing I will give things in such cases, in a sense the principle for that situation does not exist until I have confronted it and done my balancing. In a sense, an intuitionist's morality is never really complete.

All of this will undoubtedly be disquieting to many, inasmuch as the answer to one objection has hinted at many others. I think that the main, though often unarticulated, doubt that some people have about intuitionism has to do with the basis on which an intuitionist makes the particular moral judgments that he does make. Think of me, as an intuitionist, deciding that, in the circumstances confronting me, the solemnity of a promise outweighs the hurt that will result from fulfilling it. Suppose you were to ask me what reasons I have for coming to that conclusion. Now either I have a reason or I don't, and either is possible on intuitionism. In either case, though, there is an objection to be considered.

Consider first the case where I have no reason. Let's back up a bit, and see where reasons are called for. My (hypothetical) intuitionistic idea is that beyond certain levels of hurt (the level being different for different kinds of hurt), where a promise is merely gratuitous and unilateral its binding force is not sufficient to outweigh the hurt, but where a promise is solemn, its binding force is sufficient to outweigh greater levels of hurt (though not without limit). This is not a moral rule or principle, of course; it is a summation of the particular moral judgments I make in concrete cases. Now suppose you ask me *why* I treat these cases differently. Well, I undeniably do have a reason for this—I treat them differently because in one case the promise is solemn and in the other it isn't. But suppose you press on, asking me why I distinguish the cases on this basis. Now I might answer: because solemn promises just do outweigh (are more important than) hurts of only this magnitude (whereas non-solemn promises don't outweigh such hurts, and hurts of greater magnitude are not outweighed even by solemn promises). You, I take it, will be dissatisfied with this answer, and I, in turn, want to know what sort of reason you will find satisfactory.

The dynamics of the anti-intuitionist's position on this leads in the following direction. Suppose I give you a further reason why solemn promises outweigh one range of hurts but not another. Call this reason R_1. Now suppose another situation arises, perhaps on an entirely different matter—for example, I must choose between telling a lie and doing an injustice—and I say that with respect to certain sorts of injustice telling a lie is all right, but not with respect to other sorts of injustice. Again, my reason for treating cases differently may be that a particular sort of injustice is involved in one but not the other, and it's a worse injustice. And again you ask me for a further reason for this difference, and I give you one—call it R_2. Things are getting a little abstract at this point, and I won't try to give examples of R_1 and R_2. But we will suppose that they are different sorts of reasons, and also that there might be others—R_3, R_4, etc.

Now suppose that yet another case comes up, in which R_1 and R_2 come into conflict, and I tell you that in that case R_1 prevails. My reason for treating the case as I do is that it involves R_1, but if certain features of the case had been different, I would have treated it differently because of R_2. But once more you, who like to ask a lot of questions, ask for a further reason for this difference.

I take it that you will be satisfied only when the further reasons that I give turn out to be the same. That is, you won't be content until I have identified an ultimate, or final, reason, one that can be used as a touchstone by which to rank, and thus (in principle) to resolve, all possible cases. Let's be clear about this. The hypothetical intuitionist I have outlined (that is, me) does rank situations relative to one another. I do it by determining which are the weightiest features of each situation, but in some cases one sort of feature might be the weightiest, though not in other cases. I am, of course, consistent. If I treat cases differently, I do so because I think the weights different; if I think them the same, I treat the cases the same; and if I am inconsistent, I correct my judgments. The anti-intuition-ist is pretty much the same, except that he insists that there be some one final reason which ultimately serves to distinguish all of the cases that are treated differently.

And now the question is, of course, why there must be such a consideration. If the anti-intuitionist can convince us that there is one, so be it. But it's quite a different thing to insist at the beginning that there must be one, and thus to take it as a condition of adequacy for an ethical theory. Are there any reasons why we should be inclined in this way, when it seems on the face of it so counter-intui-tive? There is, to be sure, a certain intellectual-aesthetic appeal in order and simplicity, but there is no reason to turn this into a commitment to a moral theory exhibiting these properties.* One can push too far the idea that a moral theory is to be *constructed*.

*Sidgwick seems to me to make a related sort of claim for ultimate principles. In *The Methods of Ethics* (Dover edition, 1966), he identifies and prefers a variety of intuitionism which he calls Philosophical: People, he says, are able to identify by intuition a variety of moral axioms, which they use successfully in determining what is right and wrong. But these cannot

There is, however, another matter in this general constellation of concerns, having to do with the nature of an ethical theory, that must be looked into. Before that, however, we should return to the problem raised a couple of pages back, concerning whether an intuitionist has further reasons for any of the particular moral judgments he makes. Suppose I do have a reason. What then?

First of all, it is important to see that an intuitionist can give reasons for his particular moral judgment—he does not *have* to say merely that he treats this case differently from that because the first involves a solemn promise whereas the second doesn't, and solemn promises just do outweigh hurts of the magnitude in question. But the reasons the intuitionist gives are reasons only in the sense that they help us to understand why the intuitionist weighs things as he does; they do not amount to, or lead to, derivations of answers in concrete cases. The appeals might be to aspects of character, some personal or social ideal, a cause, a noble idea, or whatever. I might think that solemn promises are important because they connect with honor and integrity, whereas I might downplay the importance of someone's hurt not because I doubt that it is real, but because I think people should learn to bear their hurts, or because I think people should glorify themselves by suffering for the good of another's character.

It seems to me that someone hearing these explanations of some of my (hypothetical) particular moral judgments would understand me, even if I couldn't explain exactly why I draw the lines where I do (for example, explain why solemn promises are binding only up to certain levels of hurt, the levels differing for different kinds of hurt), and it seems to me also that they count as reasons. But they do not provide a basis for anything like derivations of particular moral

be accepted as "scientific first principles," and together they are "unsatisfactory as a system."

> Even granting that those rules can be so defined as perfectly to fit together and cover the whole field of human conduct, without coming into conflict and without leaving any practical question unanswered,— still the resulting code seems an accidental aggregate of precepts, which stands in need of some rational synthesis. In short, without being disposed to deny that conduct commonly judged to be right is so, we may yet require some deeper explanation *why* it is so.

Thus, the philosopher searches for "one or more principles more absolutely and undeniably true and evident," from which the rest of it, or some suitable modification thereof, might be deduced. (Book I, Chapter VIII, Section 4, 102) The foregoing, for Sidgwick, is the peculiar "aim of a philosopher," whose job it is "to do somewhat more than define and formulate the common moral opinions of mankind." (Book III, Chapter XIII, Section 1, 373) judgments. That is the important point. Not only do I not always have reasons that help make my weighings plausible, but when I do they are not really part of my ethical theory.

Actually, there is a rather difficult problem here—the problem of what counts as a part of an ethical theory. It seems to me that the abstruse concerns mentioned above—nobility, personality, virtue, ideals—are not elements in my ethical theory, for they are not the items that I identify in a situation and in terms of which I carry out my weighing and balancing. They are, instead, things I might appeal to when I am pressed to give further reasons for my particular moral judgments. The moral theory itself consists of the considerations that I actually weigh and balance. There is a tendency, particularly among moral philosophers, to identify as a person's moral theory what he or she regards as the most ultimate moral considerations (as well as the tendency to think that there must always be *an* ultimate moral consideration lurking behind one's moral judgments). But, as just indicated, I think this isn't the case, for two reasons. First, I might not have, and do not need, reasons I can point to in order to make my weighings plausible—I might hold merely that a solemn promise just is more binding than an offhand one. Second, even when I do have reasons, there is no sense in which the moral considerations I weigh and balance derive from those plausibility considerations. The fit between them is much too loose for that.

The foregoing discussion of an intuitionist's reasons brings us to a final matter, one which seems to me to be, though unarticulated, one of the main problems philosophers have with intuitionism. The problem is that the kind of ethical theory so far characterized does not provide a decision procedure. That is, it does not provide a public standard that anyone can apply and with which, at least in principle, determine the morally appropriate action in each and every case. As an example of a publicly usable decision procedure, think of simple utilitarianism—the idea that in each case one is to act so as to promote the greatest good. There is nothing idiosyncratic about this. Anyone can apply it and, if the facts are clear, get the right result. It is the theory itself that determines the result, and so it does not matter (in principle) who is deploying the theory. It is just this feature that is not present in intuitionism. Whereas anti-intuitionists say that ethical judgments in concrete cases must be in some way *derivable*, so that it is the theory itself that yields the result, intuitionists contend that there need be no further reason for saying, in a given case, that one consideration outweighs another, and what this means is that it is not the theory that determines the particular moral judgment, but the person.

An intuitionist's morality is, given the above, private in a way, but not in the way that is usually meant. One notion of a private morality is that of a person having moral principles that he or she secretly applies (and acts upon) in making moral judgments, and the question about this is whether it can really be counted a morality at all. But there is a different notion of privacy with respect to intuitionism. An intuitionist's morality is inevitably incomplete, since there are inevitably cases he hasn't thought about and so hasn't determined his weighings, where these cases are sufficiently different from others that he isn't committed to a particular moral judgment just to be consistent. So in a sense the intuitionist can't tell others what his complete moral outlook is: he has no single criterion principle to give us, and hasn't determined his judgments for many sorts of situations. On the other hand, his morality is public in that he can and will tell others, when he has decided what he thinks the appropriate weighings are. He can't, though, tell us *how* to arrive at his results, for he has no decision procedure.

It seems to me that we are just stuck with a choice to make—between an ultimate reason, publicly accessible and usable, lying behind all of our moral judgments, and a moral orientation that lacks an ultimate principle determining what our particular moral judgments should be. The former is in many respects a more satisfying idea, but absent a showing that it is realistic, there is no good reason for holding on to it and trying to force our moral thinking into that mold. For virtually everyone morality is plural, messy, and in an important way private.

Intuitionism and Relativism

Moral theories don't determine particular moral judgments; people do. They do this by weighing the relevant considerations in a concrete case. This means that I can get one answer, and you can get another, and there may be no ultimate consideration that (in principle) adjudicates the issue, telling us who is correct and who is incorrect. Does this mean that we are equally correct? I would say no. There is no reason to retreat, in the face of moral dispute, from the view that contradictory statements cannot both be true.

There is no reason to equate truth—even moral truth—with in-principle-provability, and more particularly with deducibility from some single criterion in conjunction with the relevant facts. It may be that, on intuitionism, it is *as if* there were no single correct answer, since all we have is a variety of particular moral judgments and no publicly usable basis for deciding among them. But this "as if" situation can exist and persist even with a single-criterion morality, since in-principle-decidability often (indeed, usually) does not translate into uniform agreement among people. It seems doubtful that there is a single serious moral issue on which utilitarians, for example, are more in agreement than are non-utilitarians.

Most people, I believe, think that their moral beliefs have more to be said for them than for their contradictories, and even, usually, than for alternative moral stances that do not contradict their own. They do not think that their moral judgments are arbitrary; they think of them as resting on an appreciation of a variety of considerations, and to be warranted on that basis—indeed, to be the best among alternative possibilities. For if people did not think this, then either they would not really have adopted a position on the issue in question (i.e., they would not really believe that something or other is right, or is wrong, or whatever), or else they would regard themselves as having adopted their viewpoint arbitrarily. I don't think either of these is the case. But to say that one believes that his or her moral viewpoint is the best among alternative possibilities is to say that one thinks his or her moral judgment to be correct, or true—though, of course, a sensitive individual will temper that belief with the concession that he might be mistaken and could change his mind. In conclusion, then, it is perfectly permissible to hold that one's moral beliefs are correct, and supported by reason, even in the absence of a publicly usable standard that (in principle) leads to that particular moral judgment.

7

Rights Against Society

Thus far I have rejected the idea that a moral theory must have a particular orientation—in particular, an ultimate and overriding moral concern (chapter 6). And I have rejected the often related idea that, from the standpoint of rights, the appropriate question to ask is: what's the best sort of system of rights (institutionalized or otherwise) to establish in order to realize a given ultimate end. (This argument has been made particularly with respect to utilitarianism—see chapter 2.) On the other hand, it has been argued that there is at least some significant continuity between principles addressed to individuals independent of a social structure, and principles addressed to social structures or to people within them (chapter 5). Thus, it has been argued that people are sometimes required to come forward for the benefit of others (i.e., there are sometimes rights to beneficence), though the question of whether there should be any sort of enforcement with respect to this has not been addressed (see chapter 8).

The central question in this chapter extends to the social sphere the question of the duty to come forward for the benefit of others. The question is: does the collective society ever owe anything (especially economic resources) to an individual that no particular person in the society owes? This is, I take it, a question which divides conservative and liberal social theorists. Conservatives, as I understand them, think that society as a whole owes the individual little or nothing, whereas liberals think society owes the individual at least something and perhaps quite a lot. It is important, however, to distinguish the question of what a society owes an individual, that an individual can insist upon as his due, from the question of what a good society would do for people, which of course might be considerably more than it owes. It might be that many liberals are arguing only that we should promote a good society, and not that society owes individuals the resources that a good society would provide. Other liberals, on the other hand, seem to think that a great deal is owed to individuals.

Among the rights that have been claimed against society are the right to equal treatment, the right to due process, the right to protection against a variety of harms (and sometimes offenses), the right to health care, the right to an education, and the right to decent housing. The first two rights on this list are not problematic—for if the organized society is to do certain things, there are certainly constraints on what may be done, and by what means. But the rest of these purported rights are problematic, for the claim is that the organized society must be forthcoming in these respects even if no individual must be forthcoming and even if most people don't want the society to deal with these matters.

There are, it is true, rights to beneficence in some cases, and sometimes such rights can involve health care, protection, or whatever. Thus, if you must immediately have a dose of some medicine or you will die, and I have some which at the moment I can spare, you might be justified in insisting that I give you some. But this is a far cry from your having a right to my doing this on a regular basis. Whatever your problems, absent some special relationship between us you are not justified in insisting that I come forward if my doing so would regularly and systematically cut into my attempts to live my life. The purported right to health care, however, is a right not merely to aid in emergencies, but to aid in chronic cases, and indeed, it is often thought of as a right to general health maintenance. So if there is such a right, it must be a right against the collective society, and not (absent special relations) a right against any individual.

The question, then, is whether there are such rights, and I take it that it is necessary to argue for such rights, not against them—that is, I take it that if such rights can't be defended, then they don't exist, rather than it being the case that they can be taken to exist if we can't show that they don't. I would not pretend that there is not a moral predilection built into this—it just seems plausible to suppose that if people (individually or collectively) are to be imposed upon, to be required to come forward for the benefit of others, then we should have to show why such an imposition is legitimate. I suppose that this is the moral analogue of an Aristotelian rather than a Newtonian theory of motion—a presumption that there is no reason to move oneself for others unless one is shown why one should (or more impressively, must) move.

So far there is probably no serious dispute between liberals and conservatives. But a serious dispute does arise over the question of whether the principles to which we subscribe must be historical or ahistorical, or whether there are roles to be played by both sorts of principles. This distinction among moral-social principles has recently been elucidated by Robert Nozick in his book *Anarchy, State, and Utopia*. Ahistorical principles are those that tell us to determine who has what rights by looking at the actual levels of people's holdings at any given moment. A principle of need, for example, establishes claims based on people's needs, usually quite irrespective of how they came to be needy. Principles of equality, again, look at how things are distributed at a given moment and press claims accordingly. Utilitarianism likewise looks at how things are and makes its recommendations on the basis of how things would be if certain claims were recognized. Historical principles, by contrast, are concerned with how people came to have what they do. The position is that the histories of some holdings support claims which at the least must be weighed against the claims supported by ahistorical principles, and at the most preclude the possibility of any ahistorical principles being legitimate. Nozick is a partisan of historical principles which he characterizes as principles of entitlement: one is entitled to holdings he has acquired either in accordance with the principles of justice in acquisition, or in accordance with the principle of justice in transfer (if acquired from someone entitled to the holding), and there are principles of rectification in case some holdings are acquired in violation of either of those. (Nozick, 1974, 151) These principles, according to Nozick, support virtually absolute claims, and it is his view that no ahistorical principles are compatible with these claims, and hence all such principles are illegitimate. Further, Nozick argues that applications of principles of entitlement preserve justice.

Nozick's argument for his principles is grounded in the idea of a state of nature. It is a theme of Nozick's, discussed earlier in this book, that there must be continuity between moral-social principles that apply to people in and out of society. That is, if certain principles are to apply to people in a social situation, then either they must also apply in non-social situations, or else there must be a significant difference between the two situations such that new principles (or perhaps new applications of the same principles) come into play. It is Nozick's view that neither of these is the case, and that the principles of entitlement that prevail in a non-social situation apply in contemporary social life as well.

Nozick's argument thus has four parts. First, there is the description of the state of nature; second, the argument regarding the rights existing in the state of nature; third, the continuity thesis; and fourth, the argument that there is no morally significant difference between the state of nature and the social state, such that different principles are applicable to the latter. The second of these was discussed in chapter 5 and earlier in this chapter, no fault having been found with Nozick's views as regards rights against the collective society. The third part—the continuity thesis—was also discussed in chapter 5, and accepted. In this chapter the first and fourth parts of the argument will be taken up. First we will take up claims that state of nature scenarios like Nozick's are inappropriate bases for generating moral-political principles. Later we take up the question of whether there are significant differences between state of nature and social life.

Uses of the Idea of the State of Nature

We begin by taking up the idea of a state of nature. Nozick is not the only philosopher to use this idea—it is familiar in social contract theories. It will be useful to contrast Nozick's idea of a state of nature with Rawls's, though what follows will not be an exercise in textual scrutiny. It is an outline of their views, on the impressionistic side, both for the sake of readers not familiar with them, and to make clear the elements of their theories on which I would like to focus.

The idea of a state of nature is usually found in social contract theories. But though both Rawls and Nozick theorize from the perspective of a state of nature, only Rawls has a contract theory; Nozick makes a rather different use of (his conception of) the state of nature. Let's begin by describing briefly a typical contractarian line of thought, and then see how Rawls and Nozick deal with states of nature. A typical contract argument goes as follows: Initially people lived in a state of nature, variously described as a world without political order, or without either political order or moral rules, or something like that. Different philosophers have had different ideas about human nature, about what constraints (moral or otherwise) exist in a state of nature, and about the extent to which there can be social life in such a state, but however they conceive of it, and whatever good elements there may be in it, it turns out in the end that it's not the most favorable situation for people to live in. People in such a state come to see that they would be better off getting out of it, and this leads all or most of them to enter into some sort of general agreement whereby they each give up something (some right or liberty) either in exchange for similar concessions on the part of others, or for others' taking on certain obligations, the result of which is expected to be a better life for everyone. Some philosophers have thought that such a contract underlies morality, others that it accounts for the foundation of society with its constraints, while others have thought that it only accounts for the emergence and justification of government and for a citizen's obligation to obey it.

There is, however, no evidence that there ever was such an agreement among any group of people, and so it immediately appears that there is a serious flaw in any attempt to defend social principles, not to mention the binding force on present generations of principles supposedly agreed upon by some prior generation, by such an argument. The usual way to deal with this is to shift to a hypothetical contract theory: though no one ever actually entered into a social contract, they would have done so if they could (because it would be rational to do so), and this constitutes a basis for regarding as binding the principles that would have been agreed upon. What is especially nice about this version of the contract argument is that it can be applied to the present generation. All we have to do is imagine what life in such a state would be like, think of what social principles we would agree upon in order to get out of that state, and conclude that we are bound by such principles. Or alternatively, at least with respect to certain social principles, we can ask ourselves whether we should like to switch to a situation in which those principles did not constitute constraints on people's behavior, and if we would not, then we can conclude that these principles should be regarded as binding.

Rawls has a variant of hypothetical contract theory. He observes correctly that what principles you generate from a desire to get out of a state of nature will depend on what you think the state of nature is like. But further, he observes, given that rational self-interest is expected to predominate in making this agreement, what principles a person will agree to will depend on how he thinks it will work out for him. At this point Rawls's thinking diverges from the classical contract theorists. Briefly, Rawls thinks that the basis from which we should select common social principles which we can all agree upon must be one in which no one is in a position to shape the principles in such a way that they will be known in advance to favor him over others. Rawls thus recommends that we think of the hypothetical state of nature not as a hypothesis about what the situation of people might actually have been at some time in the past, but rather as a mental device, a hypothetical state that we can in some sense imagine ourselves in even though it is not a state that could ever exist. This hypothetical state of affairs plays the same role in Rawls's theory that the state of nature plays in others' theories—namely, it constitutes merely the basis on which social principles are projected. Rawls calls this hypothetical state the original position. It is a situation in which each person is behind a "veil of ignorance" that prevents him from knowing such details about himself as his level of intelligence, talents, or whatever—things which would lead a person self-interestedly selecting principles to select those favoring his particular characteristics. People in such a position, according to Rawls, would want to be able to make living arrangements with one another and to develop themselves as they see fit in the context of an ongoing society—that is, against the background of social institutions which constrain everyone's behavior. Of course, everyone would want these background institutions to be just, and it is Rawls's belief that people in the original position would select the following ordered principles as defining just background institutions: (1) each person is to have an equal right to the most extensive basic liberty compatible with a similar liberty for others; (2) social and economic inequalities are to be arranged so that they are both (a) reasonably expected to be to everyone's advantage, and (b) attached to positions and offices open to all. (Rawls, 1971, 60)

Rawls's argument for these principles is complex. The direct argument rests on certain ideas in decision theory, a constructivist conception of morality, and certain moral intuitions, and is buttressed by considerations having to do with human motivational psychology, the development of moral ideas in children, and the conditions necessary for social stability. There is no need for us to go into this here.

Nozick has a rather different state of nature theory. He does not insist that any society has actually developed out of a state of nature, but a state of nature is, he believes, a possible state of affairs for people, and it is illuminating, he says, to see how things might have gone had there ever been such a situation. For this might tell us something about what is legitimate and illegitimate for a political state to do, even if it is not an accurate explanation of how it came into being. Nozick does not propose that we think about the horrors of a Hobbesian state of nature; he is more interested in seeing what would naturally develop out of a situation in which there are moral constraints that are reasonably effective in regulating people's behavior, but in which there is no political order—no political *state* having "fundamental coercive power," which is power "not resting upon any consent of the person to whom it is applied." (Nozick, 1974, 6)

The important thing here is that, as Nozick sees it, the evolution from a state of nature has nothing to do with large-scale contracts— certainly not actual ones and not even hypothetical ones. Nozick explores how, as he sees it, things might *actually* progress. He imagines that there would initially be actual agreements made between pairs or among small groups of individuals. These agree-

ments might have to do with anything—production, trade, amuse-
ment, whatever, though a very important kind of agreement, about
which Nozick has much to say, would concern mutual defense. (In
Nozick's, as in Locke's, view it is the infirmities of the state of nature
in this regard that makes it desirable to institute political governance, though the mechanisms for achieving it are different for
Nozick and Locke, the latter thinking in terms of a social contract.)

At this point, some of the critical components of Nozick's argument come to light. First, we are to be concerned only with the
actual, initially small-scale, agreements that people *do* make, and
not with large-scale agreements that they might have made with
everyone. Second, within certain limits people are entitled to, and
bring to their agreements, whatever resources they have extracted
from nature and perhaps altered by their labor. All agreements are
made voluntarily from that basis, and not from the basis of some
conception of fairness or desert that is not voluntarily subscribed to
as part of an actual agreement. And third (and here Nozick is in
agreement with classical contract theorists), "what persons may and
may not do to one another limits what they may do through the
apparatus of a state, or do to establish such an apparatus. The moral
prohibitions it is permissible [for individuals] to enforce [in the state
of nature] are the source of whatever legitimacy the state's fundamental coercive power has." (Nozick, 1974, 6) This is critical in
Nozick's thinking. What it says is that a political state can have no
rights that an individual would not have apart from a state; there
are, as it were, no emergent rights. No amount of social complexity,
by itself, can alter these limits on what the state may do with respect
to an individual. And of course, coupled with Nozick's views about
property, this means that no involuntary redistribution of resources
is permissible.

To repeat, just to fix ideas, Nozick's view is that from the
perspective of a state of nature we are entitled to think only of what
actual agreements and associations would emerge on the basis of
actual, voluntary undertakings. We are not warranted in thinking in
terms of what people would have agreed upon had they deliberated
with everyone collectively about what general social principles to
adopt. The state (that is, the most august state that is legitimate), in
Nozick's view, is only what emerges from such voluntary agreements.

The State of Nature

How seriously can we take the idea of a genuine state of nature?
Have human beings ever lived outside of a social state? Could they

have done so? These are some of the questions that a Nozickean social theory must answer. And there are still others, which any social theory must answer—namely, what is a society? Does the existence or emergence of a society impose moral constraints of its own? Or, and most important for Nozick's argument, are the moral constraints within social life no different from those in a state of nature?

To begin with, we should note that people have always found it rather easy to imagine a non-social state, and to think of it in addition as a *pre*social state. The apparent ease of conceiving of this is undoubtedly responsible for the ready acceptance of state of nature/social contract theories. One readily reasons as follows: social life demands a variety of constraints on individual behavior; social life is a historically emergent situation for human beings; therefore, there was a time when these constraints on behavior did not exist; therefore, these constraints must in some way or other be of human creation; finally, the most likely explanation and the best justification of these constraints is that people have agreed to abide by them, for promising is a phenomenon existing in a state of nature, and a social contract is thus a way of producing new constraints out of moral tools already available.

This is a powerful line of thought—it comports well with the individualist's sense that a person can be bound, or constrained, only by his undertakings, either his actual undertakings, or the ones he is bound to by being a party (even if only in some historical sense) to a contract of some sort. Thus in the minds of many it is a powerful social criticism to point out of some policy that it violates the terms of the social contract.

Of course, the social contract itself is only the source of *additional* constraints—those over and above the constraints of the state of nature. As mentioned earlier, different philosophers have had different ideas about what moral requirements there are in a state of nature. We are supposing that there is at least the obligation to keep one's promises. But we are also supposing, with Nozick, that in a state of nature there are no duties of justice, and indeed, that Robinson Crusoes living on separate islands owe nothing to one another that they do not voluntarily undertake.

There are a number of possible ways of trying to respond to Nozick's argument. One is to contend that there are ahistorical principles that apply in a state of nature as well as in society. If there were such principles, something further would have to be said about how they mesh with or supplant the sorts of entitlements Nozick sees as being established by original acquisition and transfer. In any event, such a claim would have to overcome the

Robinson Crusoe example that is central to Nozick's argument. Another possible response is to deny that there ever was, or even could have been, a situation in which people have lived that was significantly different in relevant respects from a social situation. Such an argument would, if successful, not actually defeat Nozick's principles, but seriously undercut the case for them. A third possibility is to concede that there could have been a state of nature, but contend that in such a state people may not acquire exclusive holdings. Finally, one might argue that the idea of a state of nature and of entitlements is acceptable, but that with the advent of society things changed, such that new principles, not applicable in a state of nature, came into play and at least sometimes prevail over historical entitlements. In what follows I will deal with some of these matters, though not necessarily in order or by name.

The notion of a state of nature is the idea of a state that is supposed to be the opposite of society. But great variations in the notion are possible. For some who use the notion of a state of nature, all that is missing is political organization (political society). There is still a situation among people that, in the usual sense, we think of as social life—interaction, interdependence, comity, cooperation, limited benevolence, agreements, enforcement. Some writers call this civil society to distinguish it from political society.

For other theorists, a state of nature consists of a large number of completely isolated individuals or families, and many of the above features (cooperation, etc.) are missing. Here there is not only no political society, but no civil society, and perhaps no morality, as well.

Rawls, as I understand him, thinks of state of nature scenarios as being based on the latter model. Responding to this model, he holds that such a state of affairs is not possible for us, for it ignores the social aspects of human relationships. We are fully social beings for whom "membership in our society is given," such that "we cannot know what we would have been like had we not belonged to it (perhaps the thought itself lacks a sense)." (Rawls, 1977, 162) Indeed our description of individuals must make essential reference to their social character. Since we are social beings, Rawls says, we cannot conceive of ourselves apart from society; at best we can conceive of the state of nature as "the so-called no-agreement point," which is to be understood only as "general egoism and its consequences." (Rawls, 1977, 162) Thus, we cannot take seriously the idea of *joining* society, since we cannot really compare what it would be like to be in society with what it would be like not to be in society. We are born into our society; what we are is largely determined by our upbringing in society; there is no realizable being that we can even think about apart from society; "it is not optional (up to us) whether or not we belong to society." (Rawls, 1977, 165) Given all of this, according to Rawls, there is no meaningful question of whether to be in society or not, but only the question of what our society is to be like, how it is to be regulated, what background institutions there should be.

If the only question for us is not whether anyone, with his holdings, should come into society, but rather what the society and its various sets of holdings should be like, it would be easy to get the idea that Rawls's principles pay no attention at all to historical entitlement—that is, to the holdings that individuals presently have and claim to be entitled to as a result of past occurrences and transactions. But this would be a misunderstanding of Rawls. On Rawls's view people's historical claims are largely to be honored, in that we are not to think of ourselves, in applying his principles of justice, as beginning at day one and assigning goods to people afresh. Rather, ownership and other social goods are taken as we find them, but are to be dealt with by the preferred background institutions of society in such a way as to benefit the least favored social classes. One who has much property may keep it—but only if his keeping it satisfies the difference principle, and this is, at least as far as Rawls's principles are concerned, irrespective of the origins of his holdings. So it would be a mistake to say that Rawls does not respect holdings. His view is, rather, that there is a deficiency in anyone's claims to his present holdings, in that the having of them reflects the possession of personal characteristics (even talent, intelligence, skill) the having of which is arbitrary from a moral point of view. Accordingly, no one's title to his present holdings is morally perfect, and the *future* array of holdings should conform to principles of justice—in particular, the principle that unequal holdings are justified only if they benefit everyone (particularly the worst off social class).

It seems to some, however, and I include myself here, that Rawls is too quick with historical claims to holdings. For it is troubling that Rawls's principles of justice virtually guarantee that no naturally arising set of holdings is likely to be just, no matter how benign the acquisition and no matter how benignly used. Consider the following: A group of people are turned loose in a large expanse of untouched territory. Each person (or family) goes his own way, appropriates some land, and establishes a life. Everyone is at least fairly well off, relatively speaking. Some individuals, though, are especially industrious and ingenious, and develop superior standards of living (better food, some conveniences, etc). Others are permitted to trade for or purchase these goods and techniques that make life better, at fair exchange rates; there is no gouging, no profiteering, no taking advantage. Now it is troubling to be told that according to Rawls's principles this situation might be morally objectionable, on the ground that if the appropriate background institutions were in place, the least advantaged among these people would be better off.

What this suggests is that Rawls intends his principles to apply to a social situation that is different in significant and relevant ways from the one just described. So what we need is a sense of what the difference is, an account of why different principles apply in the two sorts of situations, and an explanation of why Rawls's principles are the proper ones to apply in the yet-to-be-described social situation. I will leave this task to Rawlsians; my interests lie elsewhere.

Part of Rawls's argument is generated by the observation that we are social beings. The idea is that because we are social beings we cannot make sense of our actually being outside of society, trying to decide on what terms we shall come in. But this line of thought seems to me to rest on a mistaken idea—that being *in a society*, and being *social beings*, are the same thing. No doubt, if we are beings having social characteristics, these characteristics presuppose the existence of social life, at least at some time. We need not, though, speculate on the origins of our social being, for it is not necessary to think of a state of nature as being pre-social in the sense of being a state that preceded all social life whatever. All that state of nature scenarios require is that we think of situations in which people— *social* beings, if you will—are essentially isolated. It would, certainly, be interesting to know the origins of those social characteristics, and state-of-nature explanations of their origins are probably mistaken, but this does not show that actual state-of-nature scenarios are similarly mistaken.

The example referred to a couple of paragraphs back is a state-of-nature scenario—it involves a group of people, who are social beings, existing, at least for a time, outside of society. But to have a plausible state-of-nature scenario we do not have to go so far as to imagine *everyone* in a region living outside of a society. Some of those who settled the American colonies and later the American frontier can be regarded as having been in a state of nature. And if we eventually discover beings elsewhere in the universe, with whom there is the potential for interaction, comity, and whatever, then initially we will be in a state of nature with respect to them.

Again, it is not necessary to speculate on origins. All we need are situations in which some individuals or families are in a state of nature with respect to others (who may themselves either be isolated or in a society), and then we can raise some of the important questions: what constitutes becoming a member of a society, and what, if any, rights does one acquire on becoming a member? The first of these questions is particularly important because it requires us to focus on what a society is. This does not, though, have to be taken as a question about origins, for as long as there are social situations and non-social situations it will be appropriate to ask what the difference is. Accordingly, we can approach the question of what a society is by imagining one growing from scratch, without presupposing that we are saying anything about actual social origins. Nozick's answers to the questions raised above are that a society is a loose federation of individuals (or families) joined to some but not to all other individuals by a variety of voluntary agreements, and one joins a society just by entering into voluntary agreements with others. On entering a society, Nozick holds, one's rights are limited to the rights he had in the state of nature and the rights acquired by contract. There are no rights against society as a whole—except rights against the society-wide protective agency that he thinks would emerge over time.

It has been argued earlier that there can be rights of beneficence—occasions on which one might be justified in insisting that another person come forward on his or her behalf, either by performing some act or by making resources available. Such rights can exist in a state of nature, for they are rights against particular individuals and can exist in the absence of any special relationships whatever among the people involved. Such rights exist also among individuals in society. But rights to beneficence exist only in the adventitious case, not where the needs to be provided for are regular and systematic. For in chronic cases paying attention to others' needs—even the most pressing needs—would make too severe an impact on an individual's own projects, though sometimes where there is a special relationship—for example, parent-child—one may have to come forward for another even where the problem is chronic. So, though there are rights to beneficence in the state of nature, and also against individuals in society, such rights do not exist in chronic cases. Nor does that mean that an individual in society has a right that the society create mechanisms or institutions for dealing with chronic situations, for there is still all the difference between the occasional rescue, and ongoing and everlasting "rescue", and it is not at all clear why anyone should be justified in insisting on that, whether against an individual or against a collective.

So if a case is to be made for an individual's having a claim to a collective coming forward for his benefit, it seems to me that this must be based on some sort of connection between the individual, his problem, and the collective. And, again, we must remember that we are not speaking here of what a better society would do, but only of what a society must, morally speaking, do.

The Basis of Rights Against the Collective Society

I will imagine a number of isolated individuals or families from which a society emerges. The advent of a society out of these individuals is not, however, a single event that involves everyone at once. There are modest interrelationships at first, and these may enlarge, not in a deliberate, self-conscious way, but rather by slow accretion. Ties are created, some of which fall apart, but the tendency is toward larger agglomerations. There are a variety of possible ties among the people in these agglomerations. There are relations of friendship, but there is also participation in joint projects, such as common schooling, common prayer, and protection. Also there are business and economic relations.

There is one point in this development which is particularly significant. This is the point at which the bulk of individuals have made an economic commitment to the ongoing character of the agglomeration—that is, when they have oriented their livelihoods in such a way that they are dependent on the success of the agglomerate and will suffer considerably if it ceases to exist. This would be the situation, for example, of a (reasonably) self-sufficient farmer who turns to a single cash crop and whose success depends on the market created by (i.e., constituted by) the agglomerate. The commitment is even greater if in the process his land becomes unsuitable for diversified farming, so that it has become difficult to return to the old way. The commitment is yet clearer in the case of one who gives up farming in favor of a job in a factory.

The commitment involved must not be understood to have any moral significance in itself. For one thing, it is not a promise, even an implicit promise, and it is not made for the sake of any promises, even implicit ones, from others. It is a commitment only in the sense of taking a leap with the hope that things will work out well. It is a commitment in the sense of a voluntarily undertaken dependency: one has given up something in the hope of an improvement, but that hope rests in part on things outside of one's control. Secondly, it is not part of this commitment or of similar commitments by others that a significant "we" feeling is produced. Indeed, that is most unlikely, inasmuch as these commitments are made (largely, anyway) with the hope of personal gain.

At this stage we have reached specialization and division of labor, which mark a clear break with what existed before. I would not want to identify the advent of a society with the coming into prominence of these phenomena, for something that could properly be called a society exists back at the stage of common schooling, common protection, etc. But it does seem to me that the move from widespread self-sufficiency to large-scale specialization and division of labor in primary economic activity is particularly important, and that when these are in place we may properly speak of a collective. Though I would not want to be misunderstood, I would say that what exists at this stage can be called a thing, or an entity, and can be likened to a machine or an organism. These are, of course, dangerous metaphors, and will not be pushed at all.

We should notice that as far as the evolution from state of nature (i.e., state of isolation) to social state, and especially to collective, is concerned, it can be a matter of choice for individuals. We are all social beings, to be sure (though I am not speculating on the origins of that), but we are not all necessarily in a society, and at some times some of us can leave (return to self-sufficiency and relative isolation). We can, therefore, make sense of the idea of deciding whether we will be better off in society or out of it. In modern life, to be sure, one cannot very readily retreat to self-sufficiency and isolation—the frontier is gone. But this does not color the availability of such a choice in other possible situations. On the other hand, the choice a person makes is not a decision "to join society." The collective does not extend an invitation, whereupon the individual decides whether it is to his advantage to join. Rather, one "joins"—or better, enters, or becomes a part of—the collective by entering into economic relations with other individuals. No one issues a membership card; there is no authoritative certification of entry, no notion of *de jure* membership in the collective. Membership is *de facto*—you become a member if you become a *de facto* part of the collective, which is a matter of abandoning (complete) self-sufficiency and taking part in the economic life of the collective. The collective, in turn, is nothing more than, and is constituted by, individuals thus engaged in primary economic activities.

What is the character of the relation between an individual and his or her society, in the conception of a social collective sketched above? First of all, I will assume that everyone who is a part of the collective, but has a choice about it, is a member because he or she expects to benefit thereby. This need not be true of everyone, and indeed it might not (logically speaking) even have to be true of many or even any, but it is the sort of thing we rather expect to be true of most or all. Now one important feature of the relation between an individual and a social collective is that an individual can benefit from his or her membership only if others benefit. Of course, not *all* others have to benefit; *enough* must benefit, and thus find it worthwhile staying in the collective (assuming there is a choice about this), for if enough do not benefit, the collective will disintegrate. It is worth noting that this feature of one's relation to a collective applies both to market and non-market societies. In a successful market, many must benefit; if not enough succeed, it will cease to exist.

There are, however, many joint or collective enterprises which have the feature just described, and yet are importantly different from the social collective we are considering. Suppose a group of individuals constructs a dam that requires regular maintenance. The maintenance program will succeed only if enough people benefit from it (it does not matter how many is enough—in this case it could be a minority). But any given individual can benefit from the program even without contributing, if enough others continue to contribute—this is the free rider problem. The social collective we are considering, in contrast, is not like this. While a social collective will succeed, and continue to exist, only if enough people benefit, an individual cannot benefit (or, at least, benefit very significantly) without contributing to the enterprise. In a social collective the benefit gained by a given individual depends not only on the continued input of others, but also on the individual's own continued activity. This is eminently the case with markets. Though a non-participant may gain some benefits from the existence of a market, the significant benefits can be had only by participating; with respect to these benefits, one cannot be a free rider.

Many would say that in the free rider case the individual has an obligation to the collective. But in the case of a social collective there does not seem to be a case for an obligation of the individual to contribute, for one who ceases to participate in the general economic activity will not continue to benefit (very much, anyway). The question we are most interested in, though, is whether the collective can owe anything to the individual.

I think it can. The case for the possibility of rights against the collective rests on three foundations. (1) The success of those who succeed in the general economic life of a collective depends on the continuous functioning of that economic life, and thus depends on participation by others. But (2) in the economic life of a group there are inevitably (predictably) losers. Indeed, there might be economic structures which are such that it is not possible for everyone to succeed. In any event, there are inevitably individuals who become losers in the economic life of a group, and who can appropriately be called its victims. Such individuals are no longer able to gain benefits by their own efforts in the group's general economic activity.

I am tempted to the view that victims of collective economic life have claims against the collective—for example, claims for maintenance and/or for retraining. Some people might say that whether or not there are any claims depends upon the terms on which one entered the collective economic life. But of course there were no terms. No one formally joined up; the only terms are those one has with the individuals with whom he has entered into economic dealings. Nor can we rely on any understandings, as distinct from explicit terms. For these vary from place to place, time to time, person to person. There are no understandings secure enough to derive any significant norms from. And, further, any "understandings" can reflect only the interests or attitudes of the members of a collective who are so far successful; the voices, or attitudes, of marginal members and losers are not reflected, thus begging the question of what understandings between the collective and its members should be taken to exist.

As I say, I am tempted by the idea that losers in the economic life of the collective have claims, in that others have benefited from their participation, and insofar as it is largely the very operation of the collective economic practices that lead, virtually inevitably, to unfortunate outcomes for some participants. But this is not quite enough, at least where there is still the reasonable option of retiring from the collective and returning to self-sufficiency. For it is also a moral principle of some importance that a person must make as much effort on his own behalf as he is (reasonably) capable of before being entitled to insist upon others' help.

The case for rights against the collective is complete, it seems to me, when, in addition to being a loser in the collective's economic life as a virtually inevitable outcome of the operation of its economic practices, one is virtually dependent on the collective. (This is the third of the three foundations referred to above.) There are a number of ways in which one can become dependent. One can, first of all, become dependent by becoming specialized—by developing skills which are useful only in collective economic life. Often this is done at the encouragement of others, for often it is more to the benefit of others than to the individual himself. Second, the collective encourages the development of certain traits of character, such as loyalty, team-playing, and the like, which are, again, often more to the benefit of others than to the individual himself. Further, the collective encourages people to raise their children with these "virtues", which are not attuned to life outside the collective.

Another element in this dependence on the collective is what is usually called the closing of the frontier. As more and more land becomes occupied, opportunities for returning to self-sufficiency diminish and finally disappear, and one has no choice but to find a place, however disadvantageous, in the collective economy. There is, in addition, another aspect of this way of becoming dependent, which needs to be brought out. In most societies (certainly in our own) a time comes when the collective, through its political arm, assists in the closing of the frontier. There are in our country vast stretches of land that the collective claims to own, and that are not available even for use, let alone appropriation, unless permitted by government. Control of such lands and their resources is an attempt, wholly creditable, to mediate, in resource consumption, between present and future generations. But it nevertheless serves to promote dependence on the collective. It is not implausible to argue that if the collective is going to do this, if it is going to withhold resources from present individuals in favor of future individuals, and this has the result of preventing present economic losers from retiring from collective economic life, then it should be subject to claims of members of the present generation to take care of them in certain circumstances.

There is one more way, related to the foregoing, in which dependence on the collective is fostered. A wide variety of political decisions, whatever their aim and however honestly taken, work to the advantage of some and to the disadvantage of others. Thus, how one fares is not just a matter of his or her own talent and effort, and of luck in the usual sense. It is, again, not implausible to argue that if the collective is going to take decisions that promote its own good (whether or not this is construed entirely in terms of the greatest good for its members), then it must pick up any who thereby become losers.

Kinds of Rights Against the Collective Society

Exactly what sorts of claims are supported by the principles outlined above? On the one hand, where a person has a need that is based on, or is due to, his relation to the collective, he may have a claim. So, for example, there may be rights to unemployment relief, or to health care with respect to industrial ailments and accidents. But it is not the case that every need a person has, however basic, justifies him in insisting that the society as a whole provide resources for its alleviation.

I assume, however, that even though need alone does not create rights, a *good* society would nevertheless make resources available for dealing with certain sorts of needs. This leads to further questions involving rights. If the collective provides benefits for the alleviation of the needs of some, then everyone in similar circumstances is entitled to such benefits. A collective is not permitted, even in the handing out of benefits it does not have to provide, to distinguish among its members except on the basis of their needs. It cannot say, for example, that it will provide hospitalization for one racial group but not another. But it can decide to alleviate certain sorts of needs while not alleviating others—for example, it can decide to deal with heart problems but not kidney problems (assuming there is no invidious motive behind such a distinction). Such a decision can permissibly be taken because certain needs are thought to be more pressing, or just more interesting, though limitations on resources will have a lot to do with how much is undertaken.

There is a difficult question pertaining to some of the rights that individuals have against their collective—particularly a right like unemployment relief. This is the problem of the extent of the relief one is entitled to. This question can be put another way: it is the same as the question of what the minimum standard of living in a society should be. These questions are the same because it would be wrong for any society to require or expect anyone to work for less than it pays losers in its economic life. The alternatives, then, seem to be these: either to set the rate of unemployment relief somewhat below the actual pay of the lowest paid workers, or to identify some other baseline that constitutes the lowest acceptable level of pay. A related problem regarding a baseline is taken up briefly by Nozick. Nozick discusses fixing the baseline in connection with the Lockean justification of the appropriation of private, bequeathable, property. The baseline is taken to be what a person's situation would be if there were no private property, and the intent of Locke's "enough and as good" proviso is said to be satisfied if an individual is better off because there is private property (even if he has none) than he would be if no one had any. (Nozick, 1974, 174-177) Borrowing this idea, we might say that the level of income, whether earned or as unemployment relief, must yield a standard of living at least somewhat better than one would have in a state of nature. It seems to me, however, that this is not enough. A society that creates and encourages dependence and otherwise makes it impossible to leave the collective, may not exploit the losers it has been instrumental in creating. Furthermore, even the losers in the collective's economic life have a claim to participate to some extent in the society's rising standard of living (if there is one), inasmuch as they have, to some small degree, helped create it. Of course, many other factors enter into the question of what the social minimum should be. For example, there must be an incentive to return to the work force. No one is justified in insisting that others, including the collective, come forward for him if he can reasonably help himself (this, by the way, is a principle that many egalitarian theories seem to ignore), but sometimes people make spurious claims of right, and need to be pushed. There are probably other factors as well, and there is a distinct limit to how far we can get by appealing to general principles. There is room for a fair bit of maneuvering on this question, and as always a good society would do more than it has to.

Another right that people sometimes claim against society is the right to an education. Individuals, when young, certainly have rights to their parents providing them education—both in a state of nature and in society. But there is nothing in the character of that good itself that requires the collective to come forward and provide education, and if some children are not getting educated adequately, that does not by itself impose a requirement on the collective. Of course, again, a society may want to educate its young, and if it does so, it must provide that benefit for all the young.

There may yet be a case for publicly provided education, though, deriving from the idea of equality of opportunity. As pointed out earlier, not everything that happens to a person living in society is entirely a matter of his or her own talents and of good fortune as we usually think of it. Insofar as differences among people are due to these factors, there is no case to be made for socially monitored and provided equal opportunity. When, however, the society makes decisions, however honestly, that result in advantage to some and disadvantage—even if it is only relative disadvantage—to others, claims for equal opportunity have a place. And the more the collective becomes involved in determining, one way or the other, who gets what, the more it has a responsibility to achieve equality of opportunity. The reason for this is quite simple. Suppose the society decides to run a medical school so as to improve health care, selecting individuals for this training on the basis of their ability. But insofar as the collective acts in a way that favors certain individuals socially and economically, it benefits not only them, but also their offspring, for their offspring now have the advantage not only of capable parents, but also of social and economic advantages for which a social decision is in part responsible. Benefits of this sort must be neutralized, and the most appropriate way of doing this is by providing others with matching educational opportunities. This is not a perfect solution, certainly, but it is something.

Just to indicate the centrality of the role of social decisions in undergirding claims to equal opportunity, let's suppose that all medical education is privately provided, with no public support. In this case, I think, there is no right to the society seeking to equalize opportunities. But as soon as subsidies or other forms of public support enter the picture, the case for equal opportunity is made. Even the licensing of doctors, however privately trained, by the public requires equalization of opportunity, for it involves the grant of a monopoly by the public and prevents others who might have medical services to offer from gaining any of the social and economic benefits that go with doctoring.

Are there any duties of justice not comprehended by the foregoing? Does anyone have a right to a given distribution on the ground that justice requires it, or a right to the existence of social structures designed to adjust relative holdings on the ground that justice requires it?

Let us consider principles calling for equality. One line of thought is that people are the same in relevant characteristics, and so are to be treated the same unless there are reasons for treating them differently. This idea is thought by some to apply not only to cases in which someone, particularly a public official, has certain goods to distribute, but also to sets of holdings that arise through individual interactions. The basic question is taken to be: what justifies an individual in having more than an equal share, and it is thought that absent a justification, a person might not have a legitimate claim to all of what is nominally his, and so it may be taken for distribution to others, or at least channeled in other directions. However, this sort of thinking has been rejected in the approach taken here. For one thing, though there may well be situations in which that approach is appropriate—namely where there is literally something to be distributed by a public official and there are no prior claims on it—there are other situations in which the appropriate question is not how deviations from equality are to be justified, but what justifies a person in having anything at all. That is, there are cases in which it is not enough merely to present yourself as equal to others, but in which you must instead show why you should get something. Second, there is nothing intrinsically wrong with having more than others. To see this, we need only to think of instances in which a person could acquire and accumulate as much as others have, but chooses not to. Inequality becomes a problem only when one person's accumulation prevents others from having as much, or where inequality of possession leads to inequality of influence, to the disadvantage of some.

No principle of equality, as such, operates in a state of nature. There may be Lockean limitations ("enough and as good") on the extent of allowable accumulation in a state of nature, but these are not motivated by ideas about equality. Is there, then, any principle of equality that comes into play in social life—other, that is, than the principle of conditional equality, and the principle that where the society, somehow, has some good at its disposal, it must treat everyone equally with respect to it unless unequal treatment is justified?

One principle that has been suggested is that everyone is entitled to equal concern and respect, particularly in the design of social institutions. In some ways this principle is too strong. Our concern for a person is reflected in our interest in his or her good as *we* see that good, whereas our respect for another is reflected in our interest in what *he* takes to be his good. If we are to respect someone, we must temper our concern a bit, and thus refrain from showing equal concern for (i.e., forcing equal concern on) everyone. But respect too has its limits, for what some people regard as part of their good might not be tolerable by others, and so equal respect must be tempered a bit. Suitably restricted, though, the idea of showing equal concern and respect in the design of social institutions seems plausible. But it is unfortunately not entirely clear what is required by this, and it seems doubtful that it requires redistribution for the sake of equality. Even if the phrase can be construed so as to bear that interpretation, certainly that does not demonstrate that it is a moral requirement, or if it is, that it prevails over other moral constraints. And, as emphasized earlier, there is indeed a significant constraint—namely, that there are no principles applicable in social life that do not govern the state of nature, unless the advent of social life alters things in relevant ways. So the partisan of equality must explain what it is about social life that calls for equality when it is not called for in a state of nature.

My own conclusion is that there is no basis for saying that the relation between an individual and a collective is such that the individual may, in the absence of specific reasons for permitting inequality, insist on equalization of holdings when the individual would have no such claim in a state of nature. The strongest case derives from the unequal influence on societal decisions that often attends unequal holdings. But I would make a few observations about this point. For one thing, inequality of influence is not always a matter of inequality of holdings. College professors, for example, are not conspicuous for their holdings, and yet often have great influence. Second, influence can be created by organization, as in the cases of labor unions and special interest groups. The tools for locating and raising the consciousnesses of special interest constituencies are not impossibly expensive, and are not the preserve of those with greater holdings. Third, there may be other ways of equalizing influence without making holdings less unequal. On the other hand, making holdings less unequal is in fact a way of making influence less unequal, and if all else fails it would be legitimate to consider it.

There is a rather different, non-egalitarian idea that is often thought of in connection with the idea of justice—the idea of reciprocity. More particularly, what I want to consider is Nozick's idea that there should be a balance between the value of what a person gives and the value of what he takes.* It is, Nozick points out, the value of what one takes, not of what he gets, that defines reciprocity. (Nozick, 1974, 301) The former is measured by the value that others place on something, whereas the latter is measured by the value that the one who gets it places on it. The distinction is important, for it means that I am not necessarily violating this principle of justice if I benefit from a transaction more than you do.

This idea of reciprocity seems to me to be a plausible constraint on transactions, one that operates both in a state of nature and in society. Fairness (so understood) in dealing is something that a person is often justified in insisting upon. It is owed to us by others, even though it does not rest on a voluntary undertaking. Indeed, it is a constraint on the acceptability of voluntary exchanges. Promises are binding, but only when they fall within a broad range of fairly extracted promises. The voluntariness of a promise is a significant element not only with respect to its bindingness, but, operationally speaking, with respect to its fairness. That is, that a promise was voluntarily given is often the best evidence we have that there is a reasonable equivalence, as the promisor himself values these things, between what he is giving up and what he receives in exchange. But one can be mistaken, or duped, or coerced, and any such failure of reciprocity rightly raises the question of whether there is a completely binding agreement. This is not the place to go more fully into the question of what sorts of, or causes of, failure of reciprocity can defeat an agreement, and what should be done when such a thing occurs. The point is only that there is a requirement, even in a state of nature, that agreements and dealings satisfy the principle of reciprocity, and that often one may insist on this and have a claim for some sort of remedy if it has not been satisfied.

This principle carries over, of course, to the social state. I confess, though, that when it comes to some of its most significant applications, it is not clear to me what specifically it requires. It requires, for example, that there be equivalence between what a laborer puts in and what he receives for his labor, and between what an employer takes from a laborer and gives to him. But I don't know how to determine what this should be.

*This notion of reciprocity differs from Rawls's notion of reciprocity as mutual benefit (Rawls, 1971, 102); it may, however, be similar to another notion identified by Rawls—reciprocity as answering in kind. (Rawls, 1971, 494)

8

Rights in Law

The Idea of a Legal Right

Within institutions and practices, concrete ascriptions of rights are primarily derived not from general principles, but from rules, which either say explicitly that there is a given right, or else entail a right without explicitly saying that there is one. Take for instance a game like Monopoly. Suppose two people are playing and one of them passes Go. He has a right to be paid $200 from the bank. Where does this right come from? It doesn't exactly come from the rules of Monopoly, at least in the sense of explicitly being part of the rules, for the rules do not say anything about rights. The rules say: "Each time a player's Token lands on or passes over "GO" the banker pays him $200 'salary'. . . . "So, once again, where does the *right* to $200 come into the picture? It is natural, and plausible, to say that given the rules we can *conclude* that there is a right. The rules, we can say, serve as premises yielding the right as conclusion when we add the further premise that when there is a rule of an appropriate sort, one is justified in insisting that things happen accordingly.

H. L. A. Hart once gave an account of legal rights much like this. Hart asks us to consider typical statements made on particular occasions by judges or lawyers, statements such as "A has a right to be paid £10 by B." Hart says:

I would . . . tender the following as an elucidation of the expression 'a legal right':
(1) A statement of the form 'X has a legal right' is true if the following conditions are satisfied:
    (a) There is in existence a legal system.
    (b) Under a rule or rules of the system some other person Y is, in the events which have happened, obliged to do or abstain from some action.
    (c) . . .

(2)   A statement of the form 'X has a right' is used to draw a conclusion of
law in a particular case which falls under such rules. (Hart, 1953, 16-17)

I am especially concerned with the second part of Hart's 'elucidation'. According to D. N. MacCormick what Hart apparently meant
when he said that statements ascribing rights are used to draw
conclusions of law was that " 'right' is a term used in discourse *about*
the law, used for making statements *about* individual's [sic] positions as seen in terms of the law, rather than a term used *in* the law
itself. 'Right' in this view is a term or concept used by the jurist or
the commentator upon the law, used discursively, but not used
dispositively in the law." (MacCormick, 1977, 190) MacCormick
points out that there is an empirical case against this account. For, he
says, "the term 'right' and its congeners is in fact used regularly and
frequently in dispositive legal utterances and documents." (Mac-
Cormick, 1977, 190) An example is a section of the Successions Act,
Scotland, 1964: "Subject to the following provisions of this Part of
this Act—(a) where an intestate is survived by children, they shall
have right to the whole of the intestate estate." (MacCormick, 1977,
190)

Now one can accept the plausible idea that legal rights-ascriptions
are conclusions arrived at on the basis of legal rules, without holding
that these conclusions are *about* someone's position as seen in terms
of the law. Legal rights-ascriptions are conclusions *of* law. They are
not observations made from outside the legal system, but rather
conclusions drawn within it. They are certainly not discursive
remarks, but whether they are dispositive depends on what is
meant by that word. If an element of law is dispositive only if it
serves as a premise, a ground for the disposition of a case, then
those rights-ascriptions that are conclusions are not dispositive. But
it is a mistake to think that not being dispositive in this way
precludes ascriptions of rights from being internal to the legal
system—there is no reason to deny this status to properly drawn
conclusions of law.

MacCormick is of course correct in saying that there are some
rights-assertions in the law that are not conclusions. These do not,
however, occur frequently, and most rights-assertions are in fact
conclusions drawn from various elements of law. We should notice,
in further support of this, that where a court must mesh different
legal provisions, some of which are expressed in the language of
rights and others of which are not, there is no presumption that the
former are entitled to greater weight, which is just another way of
underlining the point that a legal rule can confer a right or support
the ascription of a right without saying that that is what it does. In

sum, in practices and institutions the main function of rights-assertions is to draw conclusions to the effect that within the framework of the practice or institution a given individual is justified in doing something or insisting on another person's doing something.

Within most practices and institutions rights-assertions are derived from elements having the character of rules. One thing worth noticing about this is that the fact that a rule can support the ascription of a right is not a matter of the content of the rule—that is, it is not a matter of what the rule deals with or of the individuals to whom the rule applies. Rather it is a matter simply of the existence of the rule, at least one very important function of which is to support people's claims on one another and on institutions. Indeed, with respect to legal rules created by legislation, we and the judges must largely take them as we find them, even when they make severe alterations in the "game" we have been "playing" up to that time, and even though they may sometimes seem to come into existence *ex nihilo*. But words of caution are needed here. For one thing, rules are not the only items that can support ascriptions of rights, and this is a matter of some importance for the law. Second, not every rule that exists will in fact support a right, for sometimes conflicting and inconsistent rules exist, and one of them must give way. And third, though a rule supports a right simply by virtue of the rule's existence, this does not mean that any and every legal rule, no matter what it says, will support a right. For some apparent rules are not rules of law at all, and even some that are may still not be regarded as supporting legal rights (though this eventuality seems to call for an overruling, or a rule modification, or some other adjustment).

What relation is there between legal rights—or, more precisely, the rules supporting legal rights—and moral rights? Though many if not most legal rules can give rise to legal rights, the purposes of legal rules can be many and varied, as can the rules of any practice or institution. Most lawmaking, I suppose, aims at protecting and promoting the welfare and well-being of the populace. And some of it aims at protecting people's rights—that is, the rights they have independent of law. How does the law protect rights, if all rights-assertions are particular and concrete—must we after all acknowledge general rights?

Of course not. Laws that aim at protecting people's rights aim simply at protecting the sorts of rights that most people have on a great many occasions, even though on some occasions some individuals may not have rights of that sort at all. And so usually, but not always, there is congruence between people's moral rights and their legal rights. For example, usually people are justified in entering their own houses, and accordingly that is an appropriate matter for the creation of a legal rule, which supports a legal right. But that rule may serve to protect (give a legal right to) someone who, in some set of circumstances, is not justified in entering his own house. Conversely, in unusual circumstances I may be justified in not revealing certain information, but that right of mine might not be an appropriate subject for legal protection if in the ordinary case people do not have such a right. One thing to be clear about, though, is that for the most part it is not the case that there are differences in the sorts of reasoning that go into determining whether people have moral rights and whether they should have legal rights. Usually the difference is simply that with respect to the larger social situation the reasoning is carried only as far as what is common among large numbers of people and their circumstances, whereas with respect to actual interpersonal situations, institutions aside, we carry the reasoning to the bitter end, taking into account matters (for example, peculiarities of moral character, or unusual circumstances) that are not common among large numbers of people—there is, after all, no reason in morals to establish rules that limit us to the general, the usual, case. The result, again, is that what we take to be a person's rights in a given situation may vary from what our social mechanisms prescribe.

There are two additional points to notice regarding the relation between legal and moral rights. First, once institutions and offices are established, they bring into existence new facts that bear on our moral assessments of people's rights. Suppose, for example, that prior to the existence of a legal rule on a given matter, we would have said that Jones has a right to do x. Let us suppose further that a legal rule governing the matter comes into existence, but that, as Jones's circumstances are not the usual ones, he not only does not have a legal right to do x, but is proscribed from doing x. Now we *might* still be able to say that Jones has a moral right to do x but no legal right to do it. But it might be the case instead that the very existence of the contrary legal rule is a factor which enters into our moral assessment of Jones's situation, leading us to say that he no longer has that moral right to do x. Institutions and their rules are facts that themselves have moral significance.

Second, as we observe all around us, social mechanisms, once established, take on a life of their own, in the sense that their pursuit of their missions may be affected by their procedures and politics. The outcome is that the results they reach—and reach properly, in the complex political and procedural circumstances confronting them—may not be the ones that would on the merits seem most appropriate, though this may sometimes be a ground for criticizing those institutions. The point, once again, is that social institutions create new facts, facts that the institution must take account of in making its judgments and producing its outcomes.

It was remarked earlier that within most practices and institutions ascriptions of rights are based on items having the character of rules; this is true of the law. But in law ascriptions of rights can sometimes be generated from general principles, for law is not entirely a matter of rules. The law consists, in addition, of a number of general principles which judges appeal to in deciding cases that are not neatly handled by the rules, and sometimes in modifying judicially created rules. Ronald Dworkin, in his book *Taking Rights Seriously*, has made certain examples of this commonplace in philosophical discussion. An old New York case, Riggs v. Palmer, involved a young man who, fearful that his grandfather would alter a will naming the grandson as beneficiary, killed his grandfather. Relatives contended that the grandson should not be entitled to inherit under the will, and the court agreed, saying that a person should not be allowed to profit from his own wrongdoing, and referring to this principle as one of the "general, fundamental maxims of the common law." (115 N.Y. 506, 511, 22N.E. 188, 190 (1889))

What is the difference between rules and principles? Though it is not perfectly clear how sharp the distinction is, it is clear enough that at the least there are differences at the ends of a spectrum between rules and principles. To use Dworkin's examples again, "the maximum legal speed on the freeway is 55 miles per hour" is a legal rule. It contrasts with the principle mentioned above in the following ways. Rules (in Dworkin's words) "are applicable in an all-or-nothing fashion. If the facts a rule stipulates are given, then either the rule is valid, in which case the answer it supplies must be accepted, or it is not, in which case it contributes nothing to the decision." (Dworkin, 1978, 24); and "rules set out legal consequences that follow automatically when the conditions provided are met." (Dworkin, 1978, 25) Principles, in contrast, "have a dimension that rules do not—the dimension of weight or importance;" a principle "states a reason that argues in one direction, but does not necessitate a particular decision." (Dworkin, 1978, 26) Thus, for example, though the principle that a person should not be allowed to profit from his own wrongdoing was a decisive reason in Riggs v. Palmer, there are other sorts of cases in which it applies, and is a reason arguing for one result, but in which it is not decisive, and a contrary result is given.

Legal principles are general moral-political principles—in Dworkin's characterization, a legal principle is "a standard that is to be observed . . . because it is a requirement of justice or fairness or some other dimension of morality." (Dworkin, 1978, 22) Thus, legal decision-making in such instances is virtually identical to moral reasoning with respect to rights, as it has been described earlier in this book, differing only in that there may be principles having moral weight that are not legally recognized and that a judge, acting properly within his institutional role, would be bound to ignore. In legal reasoning involving principles, as in moral reasoning, a congeries of applicable principles must be evaluated in light of the particular circumstances in order to determine whether a particular individual is justified in doing something or insisting that someone else do something. In the legal situation, of course, the outcome creates a new rule, a precedent, which itself becomes an item that will have its impact in future decisions.

A Legal Duty to Rescue

I have argued earlier that there is sometimes a right to beneficence. Should this right be reflected in law? If so, how? and why? There has been a fair amount of debate about this in recent years, focused on the notion of a legal duty to rescue. There is, indeed, a legal duty to rescue in many European countries. In the United States, with the exception of one state, there is no general legal duty to rescue. There are sometimes duties to rescue where one is contractually obligated, or where one stands in a special relationship to someone needing rescue, but there is no legal duty to rescue a complete stranger, however easy it would be to help and however small the risk to the one who could effect a rescue.

Of course, some people feel that there is no duty to rescue at all, and accordingly no basis for the legal recognition of such a duty. We will assume, however, that there is sometimes a moral duty to rescue. But even among those who agree that there is sometimes such a duty, some think it's "merely" a moral duty, the performance or non-performance of which is "up to" the individual, and that it is therefore not a matter for legal concern at all. So to begin with, it might be useful to distinguish different ways in which, or bases on which, such a matter might be "up to" an individual. First, whether or not to fulfill a duty to rescue might be up to an individual in that it's an imperfect duty. The model of an imperfect duty is a duty to give to charity—you can choose for yourself which charitable ends to support, and, within broad limits, how much support to provide, and still be fulfilling your duty. No particular object of your charity may charge you with not giving enough to it, and no potential object of charity may claim that you must support it. Which charities to support, and to what extent, is up to you. A duty to rescue could be like that, but it does not seem to be. Earlier in this book it was argued that the duty to rescue is a "perfect" duty—it is owed to the one in need of rescue, who may sometimes be justified in insisting on it (thus having a right to it).

Some might agree that the duty to rescue is a perfect duty, but still hold that it is up to the individual whether to fulfill the duty. Now in one sense this is trivially true, and in another it is false, perhaps trivially so. It's true in the sense that it is up to me whether I *will* do my duty—but this has nothing to do with whether the law should notice my duty. But in the sense in which it might have some implication for how the law should regard it, it's false, for it is not up to me whether or not I'm *obligated* to rescue someone.

There is another possibility: it may not be up to the individual whether or not he has an obligation, but it may be up to the individual in the sense that he shouldn't be coerced. He might act wrongly, but no one should make him act rightly: it's up to the individual not in the sense that no one can demand right behavior from him, but in the sense (roughly) that others (especially society, through its law) should not command it.*

The last is, of course, a conclusion, and leads us to look at the arguments for and against the legal recognition of a duty to rescue. First, there is a matter concerning the kind of legal recognition we are interested in. On the one hand the law could merely encourage rescue. It could do this most significantly by (a) compensating the rescuer for his costs and any damages he suffers in rescuing (or even attempting to rescue) someone—this could be paid either by the person (sought to be) rescued or his estate, or by the public; or by (b) rewarding the rescuer. But on the other hand the law could directly require rescue, and impose some form of criminal liability for failure to rescue, or it could hold a person who fails to rescue liable to the one whom he fails to rescue, for the injuries that are (in some way that would need to be specified) attributable to the failure to rescue.

We are concerned here with one of the latter forms of legal recognition, though in considering the arguments for recognition we will not at present distinguish between them. There are two fairly familiar kinds of arguments for some sort of legal requirement of rescue. One is the utilitarian argument: The law should be structured so as to promote the greatest good; on some occasions rescuing another person—even at some inconvenience and even

---

*This is the view of the drafters of a proposal for a Good Samaritan law: ". . . the Act rejects the imposition of a legal duty to give aid as an alternative to encouraging acts of aid. The drafters feel that the obligation to be a Good Samaritan is a moral one, and that moral obligations should be encouraged, not required." (Miller and Zimmerman, 1966, 281)

risk to oneself—would promote happiness more than anything else one could do in the circumstances; of course, the costs of enforcement and the negative consequences of forcing anything on people detract from the beneficial consequences, but on the whole this would not tip the balance against rescue; so, the law should enforce the duty to rescue. Strictly speaking, this argument would justify more beneficence than what we usually think of as rescue, and a utilitarian must either embrace that, or else show how a rule limiting one's obligation to rescue alone is the one that is optimific. Further, a utilitarian would have to show that the benefit of a general and enforced practice of rescue would indeed be optimific—that, for example, people will not cease (too much, anyway) being self-reliant, and that the costs of enforcement are not too great. I assume that a utilitarian can make a reasonable showing on these matters, though it is always tricky guessing what the long-term impacts on the behavior of a great many people will be; a utilitarian's best case may simply be for social experimentation.

Another argument for a legal requirement of rescue is that there is a shared morality about the duty to rescue, and it is appropriate for the law to enforce the shared morality of the society. It does seem correct to say that there is a reasonable uniformity of moral opinion on rescue—most people do feel that it is a very bad thing, indeed wrong, not to help others when there is no risk. But when it comes to legal recognition, many people are rightly wary of arguments having to do with the enforcement of morals, which so often show up in connection with pornography, prostitution, drug use, and the like. Many argue that even if there is a preponderance of moral opinion against such activities, that does not ovecome the demands of individual liberty. Well, since there are some who do not share the preponderant moral opinion regarding rescue, should we not likewise say that the fact that there is a preponderance of moral opinion on rescue does not overcome the demands of individual liberty? I think not. What makes liberty so important in the former case is that those activities are intimately connected with life styles and the possibility of individual growth and development, whereas nothing even remotely as important is systematically at stake with respect to rescue. The impacts of legal recognition of a duty to rescue, while potentially serious for occasional individuals, would probably be minimal for most of us, and so the consequences of this loss of liberty would be very minimal indeed.

But the case *for* enforcing the shared morality with respect to rescue has yet to be made. One point in its favor, of course, is the advantage to those who may benefit from rescues that would otherwise not be attempted. For the rest of the case we might pay attention to Honoré's line of thought. Honoré claims that one just does not expect the law to permit people "to flout their moral duties," because (1) it seems to people to be unjust for some to shirk while others fulfill their moral duties; (2) the law is brought into disrespect if it "has set its standard too low," and this "undermines other, quite distinct laws;" and (3) it gives people the sense that the law is not a guide, an educator. (Honoré, 1966, 239, 240)

There is some persuasiveness in each of these arguments for legal recognition of a duty to rescue. But I am more persuaded by the following line of thought. It has been argued earlier that sometimes there is not only a duty to rescue, but a right to be rescued. If there is such a right, then in requiring rescue the law is protecting rights. This has a nice ring to it—it is commonplace today to call upon the law to vindicate rights, for the law is often the last resort (short of civil disturbance, at any rate). But while it sounds good to say that it is (part of) the business of law to protect rights, because we think of rights as so very important, not all of them are important, and not everything that is important is or should be a matter of legal regulation. So, what is the case for the legal recognition of rights, and which ones should get legal protection?

The case for the legal protection of rights derives, it seems to me, from what individuals may do, by self-help, to protect and enforce their own rights. H.L.A. Hart thought* that there is some sort of logical connection between having a right, and having a right to enforce that right—for, Hart holds, it is only against a background in which you cannot be forced to do something, that there is any point to someone's having a right to your doing it, and since rights do have a point, their point must be to warrant forcing the one having an obligation to fulfill it. But Nozick has shown that this purported logical connection doesn't exist, for, he argues, it is certainly possible for you to release me from the obligation not to force you to behave in a certain way, without thereby obligating yourself to behave in that way. (Nozick, 1974, 91) You might allow me to force you (if I can) to give up your ticket to the game without thereby being obligated to do so, and likewise my agreeing not to force you to keep a promise does not mean you have no obligation to keep it or that I have no right to your keeping it.

More promising is the suggestion that if a person has a right, then (though not as a matter of logical connection) he is at least prima facie justified in trying to enforce it. As it stands, however, this

---

*I am dealing here with Hart as represented by Robert Nozick's interpretation of Hart's argument in "Are There Any Natural Rights?" (Hart, 1955) See Nozick, 1974, 90-92.

suggestion doesn't deliver very much, but the following might do better. In the absence of dispute-resolving mechanisms, an individual may enforce a right only when the costs and risks of enforcement are not substantially greater than what is at stake in enforcing the right. For example, if you owe me $5.00 which you don't deny you owe me but which you refuse to pay, I may sometimes resort to self help. If I come across $5.00 of yours, or something of that value, lying on your desk, and my taking it will be uneventful, then I may do so. But if there is a risk of a confrontation with you that might lead to injury, then I may not do so, for then the costs are substantially greater than what is at stake. Sometimes, however, what is at stake is not merely the "content" of the right—in this case, the $5.00—but the vindication of the right. People often try to dominate one another, and showing another person to be powerless by withholding something that is his due can be a way, however perverse, of doing this. So sometimes it can be important to vindicate one's right not because its content is so important, but because one's status is. Consider, finally, the following situation, having to do with the problem of what is at stake. A finance company may hold a note secured by an automobile, and when there is a default on the note, may want to repossess the car. This is often accomplished by going around at night, opening the locked car, and driving it off. There is certainly in such situations the risk of confrontation that might lead to injury, and this might be substantially greater than the value of the automobile. But though this may be true for individual repossessions, a finance company's survival may be dependent on being able to repossess, and so what is at stake may be more than a single loan or the value of a single automobile.

Now, if the foregoing represents what an individual may do to protect and enforce his own rights, then it is plausible to extend this to what an individual may ask others to help him do, for there is no special reason why self-help must strictly be limited to what one does by oneself, with no aid. It is only a modest extension of this to the establishment of social mechanisms, with their impartiality and regularity of procedure, for dealing with the sorts of cases that arise regularly. (This does not mean, though, that social mechanisms (i.e., the law) must deal with everything with respect to which there are rights, for some matters, such as ordinary social promises, may be too trivial for social mechanisms to deal with, either because what is at stake is usually so little, or because an inquiry would intrude too much into the most petty details of people's social relations, or because it is just not worth devoting social resources to such matters.)

If, then, there is a case for the legal protection or enforcement of rights, we can ask how the right to beneficence should stand vis-a-vis the law: is it the sort of right that the law should take notice of? and if so, in what way should it be recognized, what sort of protection or enforcement should be provided?

As to the first question, there seems to be a good case for the law's taking notice of this, for important interests are at stake—life and health, which are interests already protected in so many other areas of law.

But the sorts of protection that the law should give to rights of beneficence is a much more difficult matter. One obvious suggestion, advanced in many recent proposals, is that a person who is required to attempt to rescue another and fails to do so should be liable to compensate for the injuries the victim would not have suffered had the rescue been made. There are some conceptual and practical difficulties with this, which are not my main concern, but which will be discussed briefly as a means of providing some detail regarding the idea. One problem has to do with the notion of responsibility. Some writers think that one can be liable to compensate for injuries only if one is responsible for them, and that one can be responsible only if one has caused them. Now some people do think that, intuitively, omissions can be causes, whereas others maintain that there is no analysis of causation on which omissions are causes; this is not a matter to be taken up here. Were we, however, to decide that some omissions are causes, or, even if not, were we to decide that one can be responsible for some consequence even if not its cause, or liable in some way even if not responsible, then there are still practical difficulties. One problem that has often been raised concerns the situation in which there are many people who fail to rescue—can any individual say he isn't liable because others failed to rescue? A common answer to this is that they should be treated as joint tortfeasors—plaintiff is entitled to one award, and can get it from any of them, who is entitled to contribution from the others. This seems plausible. But what happens when A negligently, even recklessly, brings about a situation injurious to B, and C fails to rescue B when he could easily do so—what are the relative liabilities of A and C for B's injury? Should the rules for joint tortfeasors apply here too? Perhaps it could be left to juries to assign degrees of liability—but then, what instruction should be given the jury, telling them by what criteria they are to make this assignment?

I doubt there are wholly satisfactory solutions to this and other problems that would undoubtedly arise if plaintiffs were entitled to compensation from those who failed to rescue them, though if the courts were thrown this ball they would probably muddle through in a way that we would find tolerable. But what is the case for throwing this ball to the courts—that is, for holding a person who has violated another's right to be rescued liable to compensate him for his resulting injuries? There does not appear to be a credible utilitarian argument for compensation. It is true that the threat of having to compensate might lead some to rescue when they might otherwise not have done so, but compensation is not needed for this—a fine of sufficient magnitude will produce the same result. And though the gain in plaintiff's welfare from compensation may be greater than defendant's loss, this will depend in part on the relative financial positions of the parties. Furthermore, a transfer from *anyone* better off than plaintiff will effect a net gain in utility. Thus, this is no argument for the one who fails to rescue compensating the victim.

If we appeal to the enforcement of morals argument, I don't think the case for compensation is any better. While there may be a shared morality on rescue, such that it would be a bad thing were the law not somehow to enforce a duty to rescue, there does not seem to be a prevailing moral notion that one who fails to rescue owes anything to the one he has failed to rescue. The prevailing view seems to be that it is an attempt to rescue that is due—nothing less, but nothing more. We are outraged by someone's standing by when he could help with no risk and at most some inconvenience to himself, but we are not outraged by the idea of his not compensating the victim. It is useful to compare these attitudes with our attitudes about negligently caused harm, where in most cases we are outraged at the idea that one who, acting carelessly, inflicts injury on another should not make it good.

There are, to be sure, cases in which people do have the feeling that when someone's failure to act results in harm to another, compensation is due. Suppose, to begin with, that I enter into an agreement to guard something of value, and I negligently fail to lock a door, making a theft possible. Here is a good case for compensation. Or suppose a doctor fails to do something that he should have done, and injury follows. Again, there is a good case for compensation. The common thread in these situations is that there is a special relationship between the victim and the one who fails to act. There is either an explicit contract, or there is a well understood professional role, and in each case the very point of the contract or the role is to identify and act appropriately in threatening circumstances. Indeed, it is noteworthy that these are just the sorts of cases in which the distinction between acts of commission and acts of omission (and between misfeasance and nonfeasance, though it may not be the same distinction) becomes a bit cloudy—is the lifeguard failing to do something (namely, save the swimmer), or doing something (protecting swimmers) albeit negligently?

But there are also special relations among people in which the protection of one individual by another is not the very point of the relation. The parent-child relation is one such. We all take it that a parent, by virtue of a special relation to his or her child, has an obligation to do things for the child that non-parents do not have, including duties to protect. And I take it that this is not just a matter of the child's inability to protect itself, for the duty often applies to a child who is in difficulty despite being mature enough in general to protect itself. I imagine that if most people were asked whether a parent has a duty to protect or rescue his or her child, they would say that there is such a duty, and that it rests entirely on the character of the relationship.

Some people would push the idea of a special relationship further, and say that many, perhaps all, special relationships are grounds of duties to rescue and support claims for compensation. Courts have held that an employer can be held liable for failing to rescue an employee, proprietors have been held liable to customers, a jailer to his prisoner, the operator of a vessel to one who has fallen overboard, a host to his dinner guest, and even one friend to another—where the judge said they were "companions on a social venture. Implicit in such a common undertaking is the understanding that one will render assistance to the other when he is in peril if he can do so without endangering himself." (Farwell v. Keaton, 396 Mich. 281, 240 N.W. 2d 217, 222 (1976))

There is some plausibility in the idea that where there is a "common undertaking" one becomes a partial guarantor of another's well-being, such that if one fails to rescue (or at least to attempt to rescue) he must make the victim whole. A prisoner is in the care of his jailer, a passenger on a ship or other conveyance is under the protective wing of the one who is in charge or in control, and a customer and an employee are charges of the proprietor-employer. (Notice that people do not have the feeling that the prisoner, passenger, customer, or employee are equally liable, respectively, to the jailer, captain (or whatever), proprietor, or employer.) In other cases, however, such as friendship, there is simply a large element of mutual expectation. People do rely on those with whom they are in some way connected, and understand that others rely on them. Absent such mutual reliance and understanding thereof, there would not be much to the jointness of a joint enterprise.

Admittedly it is necessary to push a bit to find a basis for a requirement of compensation for many of the special relationships that can exist among people. But absent such a relationship, with its partial guarantee by one or both of the well being of the other, there would not seem to be a ground for compensation. Compensation is either a return, a paying back, as in the case of unjust enrichment (see chapter 4) or in the case of negligently causing harm by a "positive" act, or else it is in the nature of making good on a guarantee. A stranger's duty to rescue fits none of these indicia of compensability. I conclude, accordingly, that there is no case for tort liability of a stranger for failing to rescue.

This does not mean, however, that there is no appropriate way for the law to protect a person's right to be rescued—for there is the possibility of criminal liability. A statute recently enacted in Vermont, which is the only such statute in the United States, is a plausible way for the law to recognize and enforce rights to be rescued. The law, called the "Duty to Aid the Endangered Act," provides a maximum fine of $100 for wilfully violating the following:

A person who knows that another is exposed to grave physical harm shall, to the extent that the same can be rendered without danger or peril to himself or without interference with important duties owed to others, give reasonable assistance to the exposed person unless that assistance or care is being provided by others. (VT. STAT. ANN., tit. 12, section 519 (1973))

Whether or not the amount of the fine is sufficient to motivate compliance is certainly open to question, but the statute does, in a clear and straightforward way, recognize the right to be rescued. It is interesting that the Vermont legislature left unanswered the question of civil liability, for it invites speculation as to whether the courts in Vermont will use the statutory duty to rescue as a basis for requiring compensation.

Legal Rights in Government "Largess"

It is now widely recognized that we live in a society that has become increasingly complex and interdependent. Many people are poor because of circumstances they can do nothing to control, not the least of which is the character of the economic system itself. Accordingly, these people—indeed, most of us—are trapped and thus dependent. We have also come to recognize that the government is not neutral in the sense that its acts either don't affect us at all or else affect us equally. Choices are made, with the result that some are gainers and others losers. It is sometimes thought, or hoped, that the gains and losses will even themselves out—that is, that today's losers will be tomorrow's gainers. But even if this were to turn out in some measure to be the case, there would still be some needs that are too pressing to trade off in this way; and the fact is that there are groups of people who systematically lose out.

Over time, these circumstances and the responses to them have led to the development and growth of a modest welfare state, which seeks to insure that everyone has at least what are regarded as the necessities of life—food, health care, shelter, education. Thus there are a variety of food supplement programs, medical care programs, occupational safety measures, programs to provide training and occupations, public housing and assistance programs, and many programs that provide cash.

None of this proves that there is public recognition of the sorts of rights outlined in the preceding chapter, for these programs have been pieced together over time by many people having different social and political ideas. Some may think that people have rights to some of these forms of welfare, others may think that a good society must provide these programs, and still others may wish merely to buy off dissent and forestall potential social upheaval. Thus, in a democracy, what social welfare programs exist will be largely a matter of what can be won in the political struggle, and what emerges may be a patchwork with no discernible rationale.

So the situation is this: On the one hand, there is no legal right deriving directly from the Constitution to a job or a minimum standard of living. On the other hand, there are a variety of statutes conferring benefits on a great many people, and in a variety of other ways affecting important elements of the welfare and well being of many. And now our question is: when such statutes exist, what legal rights do people have in connection with them? Interesting questions regarding the legal status of these benefits have arisen under the due process clauses of the fifth and fourteenth amendments to the Constitution, which collectively say that neither the Federal nor state governments may deprive anyone of life, liberty, or property without due process of law. The issue with respect to the statutes alluded to above is, what counts as property for purposes of due process? For if governmentally provided benefits and other goods are regarded as one's property, then one can have more handsome rights in them, and accordingly a greater degree of security and independence.

In what has already become a classic article, Charles Reich has made a powerful case for the recognition of rights in many elements of what he calls government largess. The government, Reich argues, has grown to the point that great numbers of people derive from it significant portions of their wealth. This is not limited to those individuals who are employed by government, or get a variety of benefits even without holding a government job (for example, Social Security benefits, veterans benefits, unemployment compensation, welfare, and many other programs). There are in addition many people whose livelihoods are intimately tied up with having government contracts, subsidies, licenses, and franchises, with the use of public resources (air waves, forests, oil reserves, etc.), and with the availability of government services such as the mails, insurance, research, education, and others. The result, Reich says, is that "today more and more of our wealth takes the form of rights or status rather than of tangible goods." (Reich, 1964, 738)

The trouble, Reich notes, is that when the welfare and well being of so many is tied up with government, government power increases tremendously. A great deal of pressure can be brought against individuals and companies, with the threat of withdrawing the government largess. Thus Reich: "The businessman, the teacher, and the professional man find themselves subject to the power of government largess," and "the man on public assistance is even more dependent," (Reich, 1964, 758) particularly when so much of the administration of government largess involves the discretion of relatively few individuals in key positions in government agencies. Worse yet, acceptance of government largess even compromises one's enjoyment of essential, even first amendment, rights. There are cases, Reich notes, which "suggest that the growth of largess has made it possible for the government to 'purchase' the abandonment of constitutional rights. . . . In particular, government employees, defense employees, members of licensed occupations, and licensed businesses have felt pressure on their freedom of political expression and their right to plead the privilege against self-incrimination. Recipients of largess remain free to exercise their rights, of course. But the price of free exercise is the risk of economic loss, or even loss of livelihood." (Reich, 1964, 764)

Property, as Reich sees it, is defined by its function, which is to protect the individual from the claims of the society and the state. "Property performs the function of maintaining independence, dignity and pluralism in society by creating zones within which the majority has to yield to the owner." (Reich, 1964, 771) Traditional property (in tangible goods) performs this function less and less, since so many people's livelihoods are tied into government largess. The solution to this problem is the creation of more property, though not of the traditional sort. Rather, a "new property" needs to be created. That is, some sort of property rights in many forms of government largess needs to be recognized. "The conception of right is most urgently needed with respect to benefits like unemployment compensation, public assistance, and old age insurance.

These benefits are based upon a recognition that misfortune and deprivation are often caused by forces far beyond the control of the individual, such as technological change, variations in demand for goods, depressions, or wars." (Reich, 1964, 785)

As the welfare state has developed, there has been some judicial recognition of the sorts of concerns just discussed. We cannot undertake here anything like a thorough examination of the situation with respect to every element of government largess, but some of the judicial developments may be of interest. Early on, the judicial theory regarding some forms of government largess—particularly licenses—was that there could be vested interests in them, such that the holder had a right and not merely a privilege. But other forms of largess—particularly benefits, and among benefits, direct welfare payments more than such things as veterans benefits and unemployment compensation—have been treated more as privileges, or gratuities, or charity, than as something in which a recipient could have rights (which is not to say that government agencies have been permitted absolutely unfettered discretion in dealing with such benefits). A case which exemplifies the latter sort of attitude, and which particularly exercises Reich, is Flemming v. Nestor (363 U.S. 603 (1960)). Nestor had come to the United States from Bulgaria in 1913; he lived in the U.S. for 43 years, until being deported in 1956 for having been a member of the Communist Party from 1933 to 1939 (during which time Communist Party membership was neither illegal nor a ground for deportation). From 1936 to 1955 Nestor paid into the Social Security system. In 1954 Congress passed a law saying that anyone deported from the U.S. because of past membership in the Communist Party was not to receive Social Security. Under this statute Nester's wife, who remained in the U.S., was denied Social Security payments. The legal issue was whether this was a denial of property without due process, and the majority held that it was not, saying that such benefits are not an accrued property right in the nature of an annuity. Reich's comment on this case is instructive: "The philosophy of Flemming v. Nestor . . . resembles the philosophy of feudal tenure. Wealth is not "owned," or "vested" in the holders. Instead it is held conditionally, the conditions being ones which seek to insure the fulfillment of obligations imposed by the state." (Reich, 1964, 769)

On the other hand, in the 1970 case Goldberg v. Kelly (397 U.S. 254) the Supreme Court held that welfare payments (under the program of Aid to Families with Dependent Children [AFDC]) qualify as property at least for certain narrow purposes involving the requirements of procedural due process. The case involved an attempt to terminate AFDC aid to certain recipients, and the question was whether the agency could terminate the aid merely on the basis of a caseworker's report and without an evidentiary hearing prior to termination, leaving it to the recipient to appeal and have a post-termination evidentiary hearing, or whether the agency must continue payments until it has completed a pre-termination evidentiary hearing. The Supreme Court said (though not for the first time) that public assistance benefits are a right and not a privilege, such that constitutional restraints apply to their withdrawal, and it held specifically that where this kind of benefit is involved procedural due process requires a pre-termination evidentiary hearing. "The crucial factor . . . is that termination of aid pending resolution of a controversy over eligibility may deprive an *eligible* recipient of the very means by which to live while he waits," and his resulting need to find "the means for daily subsistence, in turn, adversely affects his ability to seek redress from the welfare bureaucracy." (397 U.S. at 264) In Matthews v. Eldridge (424 U.S. 319 (1976)), by contrast, the Supreme Court held that there need not be an evidentiary hearing prior to termination of Social Security disability payments, since (1) temporary loss of such benefits is not likely to impose as much hardship as loss of welfare benefits, inasmuch as there is no need requirement for disability benefits (meaning that the individual involved may have other resources) and inasmuch as other forms of government assistance will be available if there are insufficient resources, and (2) the kind of inquiry pertinent to the existence of a disability, being a medical question, is more sharply focused than a judgment as to the need for welfare, and is thus more amenable to being handled on the basis of documents (medical reports) without a full hearing.

Perry v. Sinderman (408 U.S. 593 (1972)) involved a college teacher who had taught on a series of one-year contracts for ten years in a state college system that had no formal tenure system. The college refused to renew his contract, declining to hold a hearing or give reasons. The teacher argued that understandings and practices in the college system gave him a "property" interest in continued employment, even in the absence of an explicit contractual provision, and that he must be given the opportunity to show that he had a legitimate claim to employment—for if he did, he would be entitled to a hearing on, and to be informed of the grounds for, his nonretention, and could challenge their sufficiency. The Supreme Court agreed that there could be an implicit contractual arrangement, and that if there was, then plaintiff had a property interest and was entitled to due process. In Board of Regents v. Roth (408 U.S. 564 (1972)), on the other hand, the Supreme Court held that merely having a job (in this case, plaintiff's first teaching job, on a one year contract) does not give one such a property interest that due process entitles him to a hearing and a written statement of the reasons for nonretention.

There have been a number of other noteworthy cases over the past several years. In Goss v. Lopez (419 U.S. 565 (1975)) the Supreme Court held that high school students have "legitimate claims of entitlement to public education" which entitle them, as a matter of due process, to some sort of hearing prior to suspension. But in Paul v. Davis (424 U.S. 693 (1976)) the Supreme Court held there was no denial of due process when police distributed a flyer to merchants identifying plaintiff as an active shoplifter, where plaintiff had been arrested for shoplifting but never tried. The Court took the view that life, liberty, and property do not include one's interest in his reputation, absent some special protection by state law of this interest that might give one a property right with respect to it. The case of Meachum v. Fano (427 U.S. 215 (1976)) involved a prison inmate who was transferred to a substantially less favorable prison on the basis of an informant's report made out of the hearing of the inmate. The Supreme Court held that, absent some provision of state law, a person has no right to remain in a particular prison, so that due process imposes no requirements with respect to inmate transfers.

Despite the indications in Goldberg v. Kelly, Perry v. Sinderman, Goss v. Lopez, and other cases, there is some doubt that the Supreme Court is going very far in seeking to protect interests in various elements of government largess by recognizing individual rights in them. Two cases involving jobs in the public sector exemplify the (bizarre) line of thought that is endorsed by a number of the Justices. In Arnett v. Kennedy (416 U.S. 134 (1974)) plaintiff was employed by the Office of Economic Opportunity. He was discharged for making certain allegations about someone in authority over him—and that very individual was the one authorized by statute to determine whether plaintiff should be discharged because of the statements he had made. Plaintiff brought suit claiming that the statutory procedures violated due process in that they did not provide for a hearing before an impartial official. The opinion of the Court said that plaintiff had a right to be removed only for cause, but that

the very section of the statute which granted him that right . . . expressly provided also for the procedure by which 'cause' was to be determined, and expressly omitted the procedural guarantees which appellee insists are mandated by the Constitution. . . . Where the focus of legislation was thus strongly on the procedural mechanism for enforcing the substantive right which was simultaneously conferred, we decline to conclude that the substantive right may be viewed wholly apart from the procedure provided for its enforcement. The employee's statutorily defined right is not a guarantee against removal without cause in the abstract, but such a guarantee as enforced by the procedures which Congress has designated for the determination of cause. . . . (416 U.S. at 152)

This conclusion, that the right conferred is in part defined by the procedures legislatively provided for ascertaining whether the right has been violated, was embraced by only three of the Justices in *Arnett*. But in Bishop v. Wood (426 U.S. 341 (1976)) a majority on the Supreme Court held that where a permanent (nonprobationary) police officer may be discharged only for cause, and the statute so stating also authorizes the city manager to dismiss employees when there is cause, but says nothing about how the city manager is to make that determination, due process is not violated by lack of a hearing on the grounds for discharge. In short, such an employee has no property interest in his job, such that he is entitled to due process protection, since whatever right the statute in question gives him is tempered by the procedures (or lack thereof) for removal provided in the statute. This is just what the majority in *Arnett* rejected. The language of the dissent in *Bishop* helps focus the issue: "The ordinance plainly grants petitioner a right to his job unless there is cause to fire him. Having granted him such a right it is the Federal Constitution, not state law, which determines the process to be applied in connection with any state decision to deprive him of it." (426 U.S. at 360-361) The majority, to the contrary, say that the extent of the right is *determined* by the process, and that the due process clause requires only that the process required by statute actually be provided. It does not take too much imagination to see how this idea could run the protection of vital interests into the ground.

This is, though, a difficult area of law, for, as always, providing full evidentiary hearings prior to the termination of any and every element of government largess could be a very expensive and time consuming matter. But not surprisingly, in light of the growing role of government largess, this has become a critical area of law, and the quantity of litigation has been growing rapidly. Courts have had to grapple with the problem of the sort of due process a person is entitled to for the various kinds of interests involved. There is, unfortunately, an ominous ring to the notion that the only "property" or "liberty" interests requiring due process protection are those created by a state's positive law. It is instructive to contrast some of the language in Justice Stevens' dissent in Meachum v. Fano (427 U.S. at 233)—to wit, ". . . if the inmate's protected liberty interests are no greater than the state chooses to allow," with that of

Justice Rehnquist's opinion in New Motor Vehicle Board of California v. Orrin W. Fox Co. (434 U.S. 1345, 1349 (1977)): "Prior to the enactment of the Act here in question, respondents were not restrained by state law of this kind from . . . , but the absence of state regulation in the field does not by itself give them a protected "liberty" interest which they may assert in a constitutional attack on newly enacted limitations. . . ."

References

Becker, Lawrence. 1977. *Property Rights*, Routledge & Kegan Paul, London.

Benditt, Theodore M. 1978. *Law as Rule and Principle*, Stanford University Press, Stanford, Cal.

Bentham, Jeremy. 1843. "Anarchical Fallacies," in A. I. Melden (ed.), *Human Rights*, 1970, Wadsworth Publishing Co., Belmont, Cal., pp. 28-39.

Brandt, Richard B. 1964. "The Concepts of Obligation and Duty," *Mind*, Vol. 73, No. 291, pp. 374-393.

Dworkin, Ronald. 1978. *Taking Rights Seriously*, Harvard University Press, Cambridge.

Feinberg, Joel. 1966. "Duties, Rights, and Claims," *American Philosophical Quarterly*, Vol. 3, No. 2, pp. 137-144.

Feinberg, Joel. 1970. "The Nature and Value of Rights," *Journal of Value Inquiry*, Vol. 4, Winter, pp. 243-257.

Feinberg, Joel. 1973. *Social Philosophy*, Prentice-Hall, Englewood Cliffs, N.J.

Feinberg, Joel. 1977. "A Postscript to the Nature and Value of Rights (1977)," in Elsie and Bertram Bandman (eds.), *Bioethics and Human Rights*, Little, Brown & Co., Boston, 1978, pp. 32-34.

Feinberg, Joel. 1978. "Voluntary Euthanasia and the Inalienable Right to Life," *Philosophy & Public Affairs*, Vol. 7, No. 2, pp. 93-123.

Fried, Charles. 1978. *Right and Wrong*, Harvard University Press, Cambridge.

Golding, Martin. 1978. "The Concept of Rights: A Historical Sketch," in Elsie and Bertram Bandman (eds.), *Bioethics and Human Rights*, Little, Brown & Co., Boston, pp. 44-50.

Gray, John Chipman. 1921. *The Nature and Sources of the Law*, Beacon Press, Boston.

Grice, G. R. 1967. *The Grounds of Moral Judgement*, Cambridge University Press, Cambridge.

Hart, H. L. A. 1953. *Definition and Theory in Jurisprudence*, Inaugural Lecture, Oxford University.

Hart, H. L. A. 1955. "Are There Any Natural Rights?" *Philosophical Review*, Vol. 64, No. 2, pp. 175-191.

Hohfeld, Wesley N. 1919. *Fundamental Legal Conceptions* (ed. by W. W. Cook), Yale University Press, New Haven and London.

Honoré, A. M. 1966. "Law, Morals, and Rescue," in James M. Ratcliffe (ed.), *The Good Samaritan and the Law*, Doubleday, Garden City, N.Y., pp. 225-242.

Keeton, Robert E. 1959. "Conditional Fault in the Law of Torts," *Harvard Law Review*, Vol. 72, No. 3, pp. 401-444.

143

Lyons, David. 1969. "Rights, Claimants, and Beneficiaries," *American Philosophical Quarterly*, Vol. 6, No. 3, pp. 173-185.

Lyons, David. 1976. "Mill's Theory of Morality," *Nous*, Vol. 10, No. 2, pp. 101-120.

Lyons, David. 1977. "Human Rights and the General Welfare," *Philosophy & Public Affairs*, Vol. 6, No. 2, pp. 113-129.

Lyons, David. 1980. "Utility and Rights," presented at a conference in Blacksburg, Va., in May, 1980.

MacCormick, D. N. 1977. "Rights in Legislation," in P. M. S. Hacker and J. Raz (eds.), *Law, Morality, and Society*, Clarendon Press, Oxford.

Mackie, J. L. 1978. "Can There Be a Right-Based Moral Theory?" in Peter French, Theodore Uehling, Jr., and Howard Wettstein (eds.), *Studies in Ethical Theory* (Midwest Studies in Philosophy, Vol. 3), University of Minnesota Press, Minneapolis, pp. 350-359.

McCloskey, H. J. 1965. "Rights," *Philosophical Quarterly*, Vol. 15, pp. 115-127.

McCloskey, H. J. 1976. "Rights—Some Conceptual Issues," *Australasian Journal of Philosophy*, Vol. 54, No. 2, pp. 99-115.

Mill, John Stuart. 1957. *Utilitarianism* (ed. by Oskar Piest), Bobbs-Merrill, Indianapolis.

Miller, Warren P. and Zimmerman, Michael A. 1966. "The Good Samaritan Act of 1966: A Proposal," in James M. Ratcliffe (ed.), *The Good Samaritan and the Law*, Doubleday, Garden City, N.Y., pp. 279–300.

Morris, Herbert. 1968. "Persons and Punishment," *Monist*, Vol. 52, No. 4, pp. 475-501.

Nagel, Thomas. 1975. "Libertarianism Without Foundations," *Yale Law Journal*, Vol. 85, No. 1, pp. 136-149.

Nozick, Robert. 1974. *Anarchy, State, and Utopia*, Basic Books, New York.

Posner, Richard. 1978. "The Right of Privacy," *Georgia Law Review*, Vol. 12, No. 3, pp. 393-422.

Rawls, John. 1955. "Two Concepts of Rules," *Philosophical Review*, Vol. 64, No. 1, pp. 3-32.

Rawls, John. 1971. *A Theory of Justice*, Harvard University Press, Cambridge.

Rawls, John. 1977. "The Basic Structure as Subject," *American Philosophical Quarterly*, Vol. 14, No. 2, pp. 159-165.

Reich, Charles A. 1964. "The New Property," *Yale Law Journal*, Vol. 73, No. 5, pp. 733-787.

Rosen, Bernard. 1978. *Strategies of Ethics*, Houghton Mifflin, Boston.

Ross, W. D. 1930. *The Right and the Good*, Clarendon Press, Oxford.

Scanlon, Thomas. 1976. "Nozick on Rights, Liberty, and Property," *Philosophy & Public Affairs*, Vol. 6, No. 1, pp. 3-25.

Scanlon, Thomas. 1978. "Rights, Goals, and Fairness," in Stuart Hampshire (ed.), *Public and Private Morality*, Cambridge University Press, Cambridge, pp. 93-111.

Taylor, Richard. 1973. *Freedom, Anarchy, and the Law*, Prentice-Hall, Englewood Cliffs, N.J.

Thomson, Judith Jarvis. 1971. "A Defense of Abortion," *Philosophy & Public Affairs*, Vol. 1, No. 1, pp. 47-66.

Thomson, Judith Jarvis. 1975. "The Right of Privacy," *Philosophy & Public Affairs*, Vol. 4, No. 4, pp. 295-314.

Thomson, Judith Jarvis. 1976. *Self-Defense and Rights*, The Lindley Lecture, University of Kansas.

Thomson, Judith Jarvis. 1977. "Some Ruminations on Rights," *Arizona Law Review*, Vol. 19, pp. 45-60.

Thomson, Judith Jarvis. 1980. "Rights and Compensation," *Nous*, Vol. 14, No. 1, pp. 3-15.

Index

Absolute rights, 11–13, 40,102
Actual rights, 36–37, 39, 40, 41. *See also* Particular rights; Special rights
Animals, rights of, 14, 15
Arnett v. Kennedy, 140–41

Babies, rights of, 14, 15
Balancing. *See* Weighing
Becker, Lawrence, 56
Beneficence
    duty of, 29, 73–78
    right to, 65, 67, 70, 77–80, 100, 101, 111, 127, 132
    See also Duty to rescue
Benefit theory of rights, 16–19
Bentham, Jeremy, 18, 50
Bishop v. Wood, 141
Board of Regents v. Roth, 139
Boomer v. Atlantic Cement Company, 58
Brandt, Richard, 45

Catastrophe and rights, 12–13
Claim-rights, 8, 10–11, 16, 35, 39, 42
Claim theory of rights, 15–18
Coherence approach to morality, 86–88, 90
Compensation
    rights and, 51–59
    principles governing, 56–57, 59–64, 79, 132–35
Conclusory role of rights, 39–41, 123–24, 126–27. *See also* Justificatory role of rights
Concrete rights. *See* Actual rights
Conferring rights by assuming responsibility, 66, 75–76

Conflicts of rights, 34-39
Constitutional rights, 1, 15, 65, 78, 136, 138–42
Continuity-of-rights thesis, 66–68, 73, 100, 102, 103, 120
Correlativity of rights and duties
    correlativity theses, moral, 6
    correlativity thesis, logical, 6–8, 19, 23–25, 77
Costs, rights and, 13, 23, 32, 69, 70, 80, 129

Directly created obligations, 48–49
Due process of law, 136, 138–42
Duty to rescue, 49, 69, 74, 128
    in law, 79–80, 127–35
Dworkin, Ronald, 73, 84, 86, 90–91, 126–27

Economic analysis, 31–33
Entitlement theory of rights, 17
Entrenchment (institutionalization) of rules, 21–23, 25, 27, 31, 44–45, 100. *See also* Utilitarianism and rights
Equality, 102, 118–21
    of opportunity, 118–19

Farwell v. Keaton, 134
Feinberg, Joel, 3–6, 7, 10, 11, 15–17, 35, 51–53, 77
Flemming v. Nestor, 138
Fried, Charles, 12, 68–69, 70, 71, 73

General rights, 17–18, 37, 40–42, 66, 70, 71, 73, 76–77, 78, 79. *See also* Particular rights
Goldberg v. Kelly, 138–39, 140

146

Good Samaritanism, 66, 69, 128*n*
Goss v. Lopez, 140
Gray, John Chipman, 14

Hart, H. L. A., 13–15, 18, 41, 122–23, 130
Henry Fonda example, 66, 69, 76–77
Historical role of rights, 1–3, 18
Historicism and rights, 2
Hohfeld, Wesley Newcomb, 9, 42
Honoré, A. M., 74, 130

Immunities, 15, 16, 55
Indirectly created obligations, 48–49
Infringement theory of rights, 35, 40, 51–61
In personam right, 41–42
In rem right, 41–42
Institutionalization of rules. *See* Entrenchment of rules
Intuitionism. *See* Pluralism, moral
Intuitions in morals, 88, 89, 105

Justice, rights and, 66, 68, 72, 119, 121
Justificatory role of rights, 40–41, 66, 70, 71, 73, 77. *See also* Conclusory role of rights

Legal rights, 13–14, 18, 19, 31–32, 54, 78, 80, 122–42
relation to moral rights, 124–26
Legal rules, 122–27. *See also* Principles
Liberal rights, 28, 30–31, 100–01
Liberties, 8–11, 16, 24–25, 35, 39, 41, 42, 46, 86, 87, 105
and right not to be interfered with, 8–10, 24–25
as rights, 8–10, 16, 25
Locke, John, 106, 117, 119
Lyons, David, 18–19, 26, 44

Mackie, J. L., 38, 39
MacCormick, D. N., 15, 19, 123
Manifesto sense of right, 16, 17
Matthews v. Eldridge, 139
McCloskey, H. J., 17, 78
Meachum v. Fano, 140, 141–42
Mill, John Stuart, 20, 29, 44–45
Minimum standard of living, 117, 136

Monopoly, rules of, 22, 84, 122
Moral coercion, 46–48
Moral reasoning, role of rights in, 38, 39–40, 52, 57, 59, 69–70, 76–77
Moral relativism, 98–99
Morals, enforcement of, 129–30, 133
Moral theories
as consisting of principles, 83–84, 85, 91, 93–94
as consisting of sets of rules, 81
conditions of adequacy of, 27–28, 81, 89, 90, 95, 97, 100
Morris, Herbert, 35, 36

Nagel, Thomas, 72
Natural rights, 2, 71, 72
Negative rights, 65
New Motor Vehicle Board of California v. Orrin v. Fox Co., 142
Nowheresville, 3–6
Nozick, Robert, 12, 66–68, 69, 70, 71, 102–8, 111, 117, 121, 130

Obligation. *See* Directly created obligations; Indirectly created obligations; Ought and obligation
Ought and obligation, 42–48

Particular rights, 40–42. *See also* Actual rights; Special rights
Paul v. Davis, 140
Perry v. Sinderman, 139, 140
Personhood, rights and, 13, 71
Pluralism
moral, 81, 83, 85, 90–99
social, 30
Positive rights, 10, 65, 66, 68–69, 79
Posner, Richard, 32–33
Powers, 16, 55
Prima facie duty, 34, 81–84
Prima facie rights, 11, 34–40, 70
Principles
distinguished from rules, 84, 91, 126–27
in law, 126–27
Property rights, 11, 34, 55–59, 117, 136, 137, 139–41
"new" property, 137

Rawls, John, 25, 72, 85, 86–89, 103–5, 108–10, 121*n*

Reciprocity, 121
Redundance of rights, 7–8, 19, 39
Reflective equilibrium, 87–89
Reich, Charles, 136–38
Riggs v. Palmer, 126
Right of privacy, 22, 31–33, 34–35, 36, 37, 54–55
Right to equal concern and respect, 73, 120
Rights
  against society, 67, 71, 80, 100–01, 111, 114–15, 116–21, 136
  as anarchical, 50
  and benefits, 15, 16, 17–18, 29
  and consequences of actions, 12, 37, 38–39, 77
  enforcement of, 130–32
  and interests, 38–39, 79
  and oughts, 46–50
  and the self, 47
  in society, 66, 67, 68, 70, 71, 111
  packages, 11
  that are also duties, 15, 16
  that one ought not to exercise or insist upon, 26, 28–29, 40, 42, 46, 49, 50, 74, 76, 77–78
Robinson Crusoe example, 66, 67n, 69, 107, 108
Rosen, Bernard, 82–83
Ross, W. D., 81–84
Rules and rights, 22–23, 122–25

Scanlon, Thomas, 22, 72
Schweitzer, Albert, 7
Side-constraints, rights as, 12
Sidgwick, Henry, 95n–96n
Social contract, 67, 103–7

Social and economic rights, 10–11, 65, 78, 79, 136
Social collective, 113–16
  dependence of individual on, 115–16, 117
Society, idea of, 107–8, 110–11, 112–14
Special rights, 17–18, 41. *See also* Actual rights; Particular rights
State of nature, 66, 67n, 68, 69, 73, 102–8, 110, 111, 113, 119, 120, 121
Supererogation, 7, 73–74

Taylor, Richard, 30
Thomson, Judith, 38, 43, 52, 53, 57, 60, 61, 66, 76, 77
Tort liability, 80, 132–35
Triviality and rights, 12–13

Ultimate moral principles, 59–60, 91, 95, 98, 100
Unjust enrichment, 61–63
Utilitarianism, 44, 47, 48, 85, 97, 100, 102, 128–29, 133
  and rights, 20–33, 39

Value of rights, 3–6, 46–47

Waiver of rights, 15, 16, 19
Weighing (balancing)
  of features of situations, 93–97, 98
  of principles, 84–85, 87
  of rights, 37–39, 70
  of rules, 82
Will theory of rights, 13–15, 16, 18
William of Ockham, 2